Crime, Media, and Reality

Crime, Media, and Reality

Examining Mixed Messages about Crime and Justice in Popular Media

Venessa Garcia and Samantha G. Arkerson

ROWMAN & LITTLEFIELD
Lanham • Boulder • New York • London

Published by Rowman & Littlefield
A wholly owned subsidiary of The Rowman & Littlefield Publishing Group, Inc.
4501 Forbes Boulevard, Suite 200, Lanham, Maryland 20706
www.rowman.com

Unit A, Whitacre Mews, 26–34 Stannary Street, London SE11 4AB

British Library Cataloguing in Publication Information Available

Library of Congress Cataloging-in-Publication Data

978-1-4422-6081-8 (cloth)
978-1-4422-6082-5 (electronic)

♾️™ The paper used in this publication meets the minimum requirements of American National Standard for Information Sciences—Permanence of Paper for Printed Library Materials, ANSI/NISO Z39.48–1992.

Printed in the United States of America

To Mike and John, for all of the love and support they give us.

Contents

Acknowledgments

This book was conceptualized many years ago. However, we would like to thank Rowman & Littlefield editor Kathyrn Knigge who guided us through the organization of the book. Without her insights and patience we could not have completed the project. We would also like to thank Darrell Seigler, Ltd. for permission to include his photograph in this book.

Chapter 1

Introduction

A Touch of Reality

MEDIA'S SOCIAL CONSTRUCTION OF CRIME AND JUSTICE

Crime and justice have always been topics of fascination for the American public, and media have made great attempts to give the public its fill. Media have always provided our "knowledge" of crime from early forms of news media, such as broadsheets and the penny press to crime entertainment, from theater to dime novels to current television crime dramas and movies. The media have provided the public with the most infamous and fascinating stories of crime and speedy justice. However, what is portrayed in the media hardly reflects reality.

If we were to take notes from the media, we would assume that most crime is very violent. In fact, we must assume that serial killing is an everyday occurrence and that terrorists are lurking everywhere ready to destroy the nation. We would also believe that police are incredibly capable of solving 99 percent of the crimes committed and that 99 percent of the suspects go to trial and are very quickly convicted and sent to prison. However, the reality is that most offenses are nonviolent and unknown to the police. Furthermore, police are often unable to gather the most useful forensic evidence due to lack of training or lack of resources. Moving further down the justice system, most cases involve plea bargaining[1] based on eyewitness testimony and never go to trial. Finally, where convictions (i.e., guilty verdicts or pleas) are obtained, even though the United States is more likely to use incarceration than most other countries, most offenders receive probation or a community-based sentence. Understanding these facts, it is our goal to provide a scientific explanation of how crime and justice are portrayed in the media. We begin with major concepts and their definitions.

1

DEFINING MEDIA

People often make the mistake of referring to the media as if it were singular. The word *media* is actually the plural form of the word medium. *Merriam-Webster Dictionary* defines medium as "a particular form or system of communication."[2] When we refer to the term media, we are referring to all forms of news and entertainment media in its televised, radio, and print forms. These include televised, cinematic, internet, radio, newspapers, magazines, and books. Furthermore, we are referring to mass media in the sense that stories of crime and justice tend to be received from many forms of media at the time they occur and for some time after.

In 2012, when Trayvon Martin was killed by George Zimmerman because he was a suspicious young black male, television,[3] print, and radio news covered the story on a daily basis (see Figure 1.1). The media took its audience from the crime to the arrest, to the trial, to the protest and the Black Lives Matter movement, to the afterlife of George Zimmerman. Yet, it was not only the news media that picked up the story. The music industry also addressed the death of Trayvon Martin along with the killings of other unarmed black males. Rapper YG released a rap song called "Police Get Away with Murder" in which he raps, "Black males in a hoodie that's a target to them." In response to the police shooting of Michael Brown, YG raps, "We'll put our hands up and they'll still shoot motherfucker." World News Rapper released a song, titled "Trayvon Martin Song," in which they sang,

> I got young sons, so it touches deep
> I'll pray for his parents tonight, when I go to sleep.
> Racism—it still exists
> Eliminating hate would be my one wish.[4]

Moving to print media, in 2014, Kenneth J. Fasching-Varner, Rema E. Reynolds, Katrice A. Albert, and Lori L. Martin published an edited book titled *Trayvon Martin, Race, and American Justice*.[5] If you were to do a Google Books search using the name Trayvon Martin, you would obtain 16,400 hits, with the first 18 hits having Trayvon Martin's name in the title. Social media also covered Trayvon Martin's death in depth. In fact, the Black Lives Matter movement was started by one of the Martin family lawyers using social media. But how far do these stories reach? How often do the media reach their targets, what messages are they sending, and how effective are their messages?

Weblink 1.1

For a detailed timeline of the Trayvon Martin case, go to: http://www.cbsnews.com/news/trayvon-martin-shooting-a-timeline-of-events/.

Figure 1.1. Mug shot of George Zimmerman, 2012. John E. Polk Correctional Facility. Photo in the public domain.

MEDIA CONSUMPTION

In order to understand the reach of the media, one has to understand the idea of *convergence* in a digital age. According to Jospeh Turow, convergence is "the ability of different media to easily interact with each other because they all deal with the information in the same digital form."[6] Understanding convergence in an era of mass media and mass communication allows us to understand how a news story read online can be sent to a friend via Facebook, Twitter, or Instagram. This same story will probably include links to previous reports of the crime as well as to reports of similar crimes. The consumer can access these stories from a laptop, tablet, or a cell phone at any time.

Linked to convergence is the rather recent practice of allowing the audience to become involved in the development of news stories. That is, the audience went from being passive receivers to being active receivers. Because news has become a 24/7 industry and because online media have overtaken print media, large media conglomerates have to compete with smaller media companies who are now able to reach a much larger audience than before and with less money. In order to keep the audience engrossed, news agencies have allowed them to participate in news gathering by including Twitter posts or YouTube videos in their reporting. Within the movie and music industries consumers are able to stream more easily than if they were forced to go to the movies or the music store. Companies such as Netflix, Amazon, and Hulu allow consumers unlimited viewing of movies for a relatively small monthly fee. iTunes and Amazon are two corporations that bring music to the fingertips of the consumer, and companies such as Pandora, iHeart, and YouTube allow for free streaming.

However, as Lawrence Grossberg, Ellen Wartella, and D. Charles Whitney point out, the availability of media consumption is unequally distributed.[7] As we stated earlier, we are in a digital age when everyone can link to the media and to each other. However, not everyone can afford the electronic devices needed to make these connections. Grossberg and his colleagues stress that media consumption takes money and time that the poor do not have a lot of. Turow reports that the lower the educational attainment and the lower the income, the less likely are people to have access to the internet. As a result, those people with less than a high school education are less likely to have internet in their home, and approximately 50 percent of people with a household income of $74,000 or less do not have internet in their home (approximately 62 percent of those with a college degree or above also fall into this category).

In addition to monetary capital, Grossberg and colleagues tell us that cultural capital is unequally distributed. Cultural capital is "the knowledge and sensibility that enables one to comprehend and appreciate particular cultural products."[8] This is important because many media forms require certain knowledge, such as financial news or political news. Cultural capital is also linked to assumptions and shared values that differ among the various economic groups, as researchers have long ago found. This also allows us to understand that media consumption is socially determined even as media help to determine the social structure of society.

This leads us to the question, *how* do people consume the media? People use the media for enjoyment, companionship, surveillance, and interpretation. Enjoyment is typically linked to television shows, movies, magazines, and books. However, Ray Surette stresses that the news media have increasingly joined the ranks of entertainment. Media researchers call much of today's news infotainment. They attempt to entertain their audiences while providing information. True crime television dramas (i.e., docudramas), movies, and documentaries also engage in infotainment in order to reel in more viewers. The problem is that it becomes hard to separate fact from entertainment. On numerous occasions throughout her teaching career, Garcia (the first author of this book) has had students share crime stories that the class has determined were fictional movies. Many students declare that they want to major in criminal justice and become police officers because they want action. They assume that what they are exposed to via the media is real and is the norm. This reveals infotainment at its worst, and leads to several questions. What are we consuming? Are we consuming reality within the news? And are we consuming harmless pleasure from entertainment media? There are two ways we can answer these questions. The first answer addresses the influences that media corporations have on its audience. The second answer addresses the social constructions that we are exposed to through the media. This book focuses predominantly on the social constructions of crime and justice and how we absorb them, so we will discuss corporate influences only briefly.

CORPORATION INFLUENCE ON CRIME AND JUSTICE

Similar to any other corporation, media organizations are focused on not only sharing the world, be it the news or the latest poems by Maya Angelou, but also making money. Media are "profit maximizing commercial organizations" and news media (we focus on crime news in this book) engage in "profit-driven journalism"[9] that ultimately releases biased and self-serving information. How does this work in an advanced society that prides itself on the First Amendment freedom of speech and press? In order to answer this, we must understand the corporate nature of media organizations.

In 1983, there were fifty major media companies operating within the United States. While this does not seem like many, this number allowed for diversity and objectivity in the content of crime and justice. By 2000, there were only six major media companies. These companies are CBS Corporation, Comcast, Disney, News Corporation, Time Warner, and Viacom, and they control the majority of the media in the United States.[10] This is known as media consolidation. How does this happen? According to Matthew Robinson, horizontal integration, vertical integration, and interlocking directorates enable media consolidation which in turn changes the face of media reporting.

Horizontal integration occurs when a media corporation gains control of a media market in a location. For example, today almost every newspaper in a given location is owned by a media monopoly, that is, they have no competition. The result is less detail in reporting, less serious stories reported, and cutting staff. These papers also have little choice on what to report so that the stories are similar. A horizontal integration in the movie industry results in similar plots and little genre variation. Vertical integration occurs when a media corporation gains control of the production and distribution of content.

That is, they control the content and the means to distribute that content. The failed AOL and Time Warner merger in 1989 would be an example of this. In 2001, Comcast bought AT&T. Comcast also merged with NBC and put in a bid for Time Warner. While the federal antitrust laws and the Federal Communications Commission are rightfully concerned about monopolies and how this negatively affects consumers, social scientists are concerned with the messages that are being received as a result of these integrations.

The final practice found within media corporations that affects their influence on crime in the media is the interlocking of directorates. Many board of directors of media corporations are also board of directors of non-media corporations. This causes a conflict of interest when reporting on crime. Crime reporting is big business in news, movies, television shows, books and the like. Street and government crime are the primary focus. Corporate crime is not. Furthermore, when media corporations have strong links to the government, even those crimes are passed over. If a media corporation has strong consolidation, controls the market, and owns the content and distribution, the public has very limited exposure to the true nature and occurrence of crime, even if it is consistently online. The Free Press, an organization established in order to fight for the objectivity of the media, argues that media corporations determine what news and information are received, how they are received, who is heard (and silenced), and what images are put out to the audience.[11]

Weblink 1.2

To learn more about the Free Press, go to: www.freepress.net.

SOCIAL CONSTRUCTION OF CRIME AND JUSTICE

The concern that the media controls what news and information we receive drives the purpose of this book. In this book, we argue that crime and justice are socially constructed, in part, by the media. Social constructionism refers to the idea that nothing is known as fact until it is created as such through culture.[12] For example, imagine that you are walking down the street and are approached by a homeless woman who asks for money to buy food. You feel bad and give her your last $5. Later, you describe your experience to friends, feeling good that you helped a hungry person. However, your friends proceed to tell you that homeless people are lazy drug addicts who do not want to work for a living and who prey on innocent unsuspecting people. They describe these individuals as deviant and explain that if you did not give her money, money she would use for drugs, then she would eventually rob an innocent person. Your friends have constructed an image of the homeless as drug-addicted criminals. They make you feel bad about enabling her behavior and of being a victim of a con. You start to doubt the woman's intentions. Days later you see news coverage of a homeless man who attacked a woman with a wooden stake[13] and you watch a rerun of a *Law & Order*[14] episode depicting a violent and drug-addicted homeless man whose violence terrifies the people of New York City.[15] These media images, which are certainly true for some homeless people, do not provide a reality where most homeless are nonviolent and may be mentally ill or unemployed with no social support, who may be war veterans, or who may have been victims of terrible crimes but who do not know how to cope. Most homeless are nonviolent noncriminals; however, the social construct of the homeless person as a drug-addicted criminal takes hold. While the media do not solely create images of crime and justice, because of their wide reach, achieved through consolidation, horizontal and vertical integration, and interlocking directorates, it is important to understand these images and their effects.

The social construction of reality explains that since we do not experience every bit of reality, we come to understand reality through our prior interactions, by information shared with us by the people we know, and by the media. Since we live in a complicated world, we are forced to categorize people and experiences. The problem is that we simplify this categorization too much to accurately reflect reality. As a result, people are either good or bad, criminals or victims. We do not allow for much gray area. Bringing child's play into how the media approaches crime and justice, we tend to be exposed to stories, whether through the news or the entertainment industry, about cops and robbers. The criminals are the ultimate bad guys (and in most cases "guy" is meant literally), and the cops are the heroes protecting innocent victims. Until we see stories of corrupt and incompetent police, such as Officer Michael Slager's shooting and killing of Mr. Walter Scott in 2015,[16] we tend to hold strongly to these constructs.

The twofold categorization within our social constructs is called a dichotomy, that is, we dichotomize our world. To branch out from the most familiar good versus bad, we also categorize the sexes as male versus female, the races as white versus black, the ages as young versus old, and lately the religions as Christians versus Muslims. Dichotomizing simplifies reality so that we ignore or deny anything outside of the two-category construct. As a result, we deny intersexed people who are born with biological traits of both the male and the female, and we deny levels of ages and many religions.

Dichotomizing, however, is not just a category. It is also a process. As we see or interact with people, even briefly, we place them into categories. We then place value on those categories. The most basic values are the good versus bad and right versus wrong values. Historically, white has been equated with goodness and innocence, while black has been equated with badness and evil. Throughout history, filmmakers tended to equate black (i.e., darkness or shadows) with evil and serious negative scenes.[17] The movie *Black Magic* depicts magic used for evil as black. Most horror movies today present evil as coming out only at night and angels are accompanied by a white light. Movies such as *Heaven Can Wait, Oh, God!*, *Bruce Almighty*, and *Evan Almighty* show angels and God accompanied by a white light. *The Wizard of Oz* makes it clear that good witches wear white, or near white, while bad witches wear black and live in dark castles.

In the reality of life, the Ku Klux Klan (the Klan) depicts whiteness as the savior of American culture against the ignorant and evil black man. In fact, the Klan chose to wear white robes to emphasize this. In the original *The Birth of a Nation* (released in 1915), Griffith depicted a nation with freed slaves as a nation that will fall. These social constructs throughout history equate black people with evil and crime. This social construct lives on today.

Weblink 1.3

For a detailed discussion of social constructionism, go to the Open Access *Grounded Theory Review: An International Journal* published by Sociology Press at: http://groundedtheoryreview.com/2012/06/01/ what-is-social-constructionism/. You can also visit the KhanAcademy at https://www.khanacademy.org/test-prep/mcat/society-and-culture/ social-structures/v/social-constructionism, for a short video on social constructionism.

As we move through our discussion of crime and justice in the media we will see similar depictions of dichotomies such as good versus evil. The young, typically teens and young adults, are most likely portrayed as criminal and older people as the helpless victims. We see that while the male is most likely to be viewed as the criminal, he is also most likely to be viewed as the hero and savior. As such he is most likely to be the cop and the robber. Most recently, we are in a "war on terror." After the attacks of September 11, 2001, in which the United States was attacked by Islamic terrorists known as al-Qaeda, the nation and the media declared, both subtly and not so subtly, Islam a violent religion and all Muslims potential terrorists. While within the United States most terrorists are Christians and often use their religion to justify their crimes,[18] the media focuses most of their terrorism reports on Islamic extremists. This focus helps to reinforce our social constructs of who terrorists are, as we saw in the homeless example earlier. As we discuss different forms of media, we can see these same constructs placed on the poor, the sexual deviant, and the mentally ill.

BLURRING THE LINE BETWEEN REALITY AND ENTERTAINMENT

Media provide information as well as entertainment. The business of making money creates a new form of sharing known as infotainment. Infotainment blurs the line between information and entertainment. In a need to increase ratings, the presentation of the news is made more enticing to watch. This is the entertainment portion of the news. As news media increasingly engage in infotainment programming, we find true crime television series and reality television taking on this same quality. The viewer learns to be entertained by the news. As television crime dramas and movies introduce these familiar stories, a process called looping, the viewer loses the distinction between pure entertainment and infotainment.[19] Looping can be seen when an event is covered by the news (print, internet, television, and radio) repeatedly. The story may also be picked up by a popular talk show, worked into an episode of a popular television series, and perhaps made into a movie. Looping often leaves the appearance of a repeated and bigger problem within society. The 1994–1995 trial of O. J. Simpson provides a good example of looping with frequent reporting via print, television, and radio news and subsequent true crime movies. This looping leaves viewers with the questions: What really happened? And how often does this happen? (See Box 1.1.)

Box 1.1.   The O. J. Simpson Case

On June 13, 1994, Nicole Brown Simpson and Ronald Goldman were brutally murdered and found in the driveway of Nicole's home. After a slow highway chase on June 17, O. J. Simpson was arrested for the double homicide. Anyone who watched television was immediately exposed to the televised chase either through news announcements or a total program interruption. News helicopters followed Simpson's white Ford Bronco as it was driven by his friend Al Cowlings at thirty-five miles per hour and being followed by several police cars. Cowlings told the police that O. J. Simpson sat in the back with a gun to his head. The chase and its broadcasting lasted for over an hour. News cameras captured spectators on bridges cheering and holding signs supporting O. J.'s flight.[20]

After the arrest, the news media quickly reported on the convening and ultimate dismissal of a grand jury. Then the trial began, lasting from November 9, 1994 to January 24, 1995, and was presented by the media from beginning to end. Daily news updates were given, talk shows gave coverage, and the relatively new Court TV aired the entire case.

The O. J. Simpson case quickly took on the traits of a three-ring circus. In Ring One were O. J. Simpson with his potential guilt and the murder victims Nicole Brown Simpson and Ronald Goldman; all being presented as if characters in a movie. The crime was linked to his fame as a football hero but tainted by his race and his history of violence against his wife. Nicole Brown Simpson was viewed as the innocent white woman and domestic violence victim. Ronald Goldman was a close friend of Nicole and was portrayed as an innocent bystander who most likely came across O. J. after he killed Nicole.

In Ring Two, the prosecution team, the defense team, and Judge Ito were featured. Lead prosecutor, Marcia Clark, was often depicted as a woman out of her league. The media often focused on her clothes and hairstyle and questioned her competence. On the defense team, F. Lee Bailey, Johnnie Cochran, and Robert Shapiro were the defense attorneys most often shown in the news. However, Johnnie Cochran became the face of O. J. Simpson's defense team, what the media dubbed the "Dream Team." They were portrayed as the high-paid attorneys who would either buy O. J. Simpson his freedom or uncover the truth with their wealth of knowledge and resources. They were often ridiculed for the saying, "If it doesn't fit, you must acquit." Judge Ito was often criticized for allowing the trial to turn into a circus by allowing cameras in the courtroom. Jay Leno increased his ratings with a recurring skit called the *Dancing Itos*.[21]

In Ring Three were the Los Angeles Police Department (LAPD) and Detective Mark Fuhrman. Violence and corruption within the LAPD has been consistently covered by the media and the O. J. Simpson case was no different. The LAPD was ridiculed for conducting an illegal search of O. J.'s property, incompetently collecting evidence, and engaging in discrimination. Mark Fuhrman was the center of the criticism of prejudice within the LAPD and was accused of framing O. J. Simpson. Media reports stated that the LAPD feared that race riots would ensue as they did after the acquittal of the four LAPD officers who severely beat Rodney King.

During the chase, the trial, and the aftermath, one could find news coverage, talk shows, and movies depicting the so-called facts of the case. Comedians like Jay Leno, Dana Carvey, and Norm MacDonald were well known for making jokes, parodies, and impersonations of the various players in the case. Witnesses became advocates, book authors, or reality stars. Denise Brown, who testified about O. J.'s abuse of Nicole, started to raise money for women's shelters and attempted to back a documentary to tell the Brown's side of the case.[22] Kim Goldman, Ronald Goldman's sister, wrote a book about the murder titled *Can't Forgive.* Prosecutor Marcia Clark and her co-counselor Christopher Darden each wrote memoirs of the case. Kato Kaelin, a witness in the case and houseguest of O. J. Simpson, became famous after the media released stories of a man who was a liar and a lazy, freeloader. He made many television and radio appearances and even started his own clothes line. The defense attorneys, Cochran, Shapiro, and Kardashian, already well respected, became famous after the trial. The Kardashian name became even more famous, allowing his children to become successful reality show stars. The books, movies, and television appearances of the various players retelling their story kept the case looping. It also increased the belief that spousal murder and police corruption are larger problems than perhaps they are in our society. In 2016, the television series, *People vs. O.J. Simpson: American Crime Story*, has restarted the loop as does Box 1.1 (see Figure 1.2).

Figure 1.2. Mug shot of O. J. Simpson, 1994. Los Angeles Police Department. Photo in the public domain.

The worse crime in modern U.S. history has been a subject of infotainment. On September 11, 2001, the United States was attacked by Islamic terrorists in an attempt to punish the country for supporting Israel, the Gulf War, and keeping a military presence in the Middle East. Four American Airline airplanes were hijacked, two were flown into the north and south towers of the World Trade Center in New York City, one was flown into the Pentagon in Washington, D.C., and the last was overtaken by passengers and flown into a field in Pennsylvania. While the country, including the media, were in shock as the attacks occurred and for months following the attacks, this did not stop the media from capitalizing on the event for years to come.

During and following the attacks, one can remember that all music and regularly scheduled programs were cancelled for days in order to provide the public with a minute-to-minute account of the attacks, the death toll (over 3,000 people), the rescues, and the investigations. In order to be the first to report the latest news, journalists were known to use each other's stories as their sources of information without substantiating the facts. The numbers of victims were inaccurately reported and stories of captured terrorists were printed without substantiation.[23] Political agendas such as the "war on terror" became media agendas. The looping of the attacks, which were horrible enough, made the event of terrorism and Islamic extremism seem to be an omnipresent global problem.

Years later, we still find movies and news coverage of 9/11 and the resulting war on terror. Movies about the September 11 attacks included movies released in theaters and made for television as well as documentaries and ranged from the coverage of the actual attacks to how the attacks affected the lives of survivors[24] and everyday people. A few of these movies, most released between 2002 and 2007, include *A Few Days in September*, *DC 9/11: Time of Crisis*, *Flight 93*, *New York*, *Reign over Me*, *September 11*, *The Hamburg Cell*, *Twin Towers*, *United 93*, *World Trade Center*, *WTC View*, and *Zero Dark Thirty*. Every anniversary, while we mourn the senseless loss of life, we also hear stories of where people were when the terrorists attacked. Social media has also breathed new life into the attacks of 9/11 as bloggers, YouTubers, Tweeters, and Facebook users give their experiences and televised news programs share these posts as if they are breaking news.

In the face of infotainment, we never ask: what information is important news and what is entertainment? We must remember our history in order to avoid repeating the terrible and damaging parts. Yet, at what point do we decide that some information shared by the media is pure gossip, some information is put forth for the shock value and ratings, and some is important news. As a voyeuristic and narcissistic nation, we capture everything through pictures and videos on our phones. We post our opinions and daily activities on every social media outlet we can access and spend hours surfing information posted by others. Yet, the sad truth is that most of us do not truly understand the nature and extent of crime and justice in society. The social constructs we hold are born of the few direct and indirect experiences we have (through loved ones) and through the media corporations who have achieved media consolidation, horizontal and vertical integration, and interlocking directorates. In order to remedy this problem, we end this chapter with real crime and justice statistics before continuing our presentation of media images throughout this book.

CRIME IN SOCIETY

We have good news and we have bad news. The bad news is that there is too much crime in society. There is also corruption within justice and a lack of resources and training. This does not allow officials to adequately fight crime. The good news is that crime is not as bad as we are led to believe. We are not in a crisis, and we are not in a crime wave. Police corruption is rampant in our society but it has decreased substantially over the decades and is not as widespread as media depictions make it appear. Furthermore, we can breathe easy, just a bit, that the lack of training does not affect the crime problem too much as most police departments within our nation are small and located in rural areas that do not have a large crime problem. Nevertheless, these are problems faced within our nation and are only touched upon by the media. So let us look at our crime problem.

Official Crime Statistics

We obtain official crime data from the Federal Bureau of Investigation (FBI) on an annual basis.[25] The FBI collects crime data from local and state police departments around the country. Data submission is voluntary; however, most agencies submit their crime statistics so the FBI data cover 97.7 percent of the population. Annually, the FBI releases these data on their website providing raw numbers, rates, percentages, and changes in crime over time. The data collection program is known as the Uniform Crime Report (UCR) and the FBI releases annual data under the titles *Crime in the United States, Hate Crime, Law Enforcement Officers Killed and Assaulted,* and *National Incident-Based Reporting System.* There are twenty-eight crimes reported within the UCR but the crimes of most concern are known as index crimes. These include what are considered to be the most serious violent crimes or the violent crime index (e.g., murder, rape, robbery, and aggravated assault) and the most serious property crimes or the property crime index (e.g., burglary, larceny-theft, arson, and motor vehicle theft).

The latest year for which the FBI released a complete report at the time this book was written was 2015. The UCR revealed that for every 100,000 people living in the United States there were 372.6 violent crimes. This was nearly half of the 1995 rate of violence.[26] Additionally, in the past ten years murder and aggravated assault rates have fallen by nearly half. While most of the crimes the media focus on are violent crimes, the UCR shows us that property crime is much more likely to occur, specifically larceny-theft. In 2015, there were 2,487 property crimes for every 100,000 people living in the United States. This number is compared to the rate of 4,451 in 1996. This is a much more dramatic decrease than we see for violent crime. In fact, although there may be a slight increase in some years, over the past ten years, we see a decrease in all of the index crimes.

However, just as the media exaggerates the crime problem in its reporting or in the types of crimes it chooses to showcase in movies, television shows, songs, and books, the FBI exaggerates with the Crime Clock.[27] The FBI presents a snapshot of how frequent index crimes occur within the nation. The 2015 Crime Clock reveals that one murder occurs every 33.5 minutes in the United States (see Figure 1.3). One rape occurs every 4.2 minutes, one robbery every 1.6 minutes, and one aggravated assault every 41.3 minutes. Property crime occurs much more frequently and is reported in seconds. Every 20 seconds there is one burglary, one larceny-theft every 5.5 seconds, and one motor vehicle theft every 44.6 seconds. This is quite alarming. In fact, this can explain our war on crime.

2015 CRIME CLOCK STATISTICS

A Violent Crime occurred every	26.3 seconds
One Murder every	33.5 minutes
One Rape every	4.2 minutes
One Robbery every	1.6 minutes
One Aggravated Assault every	41.3 seconds
A Property Crime occurred every	3.9 seconds
One Burglary every	20.0 seconds
One Larceny-theft every	5.5 seconds
One Motor Vehicle Theft every	44.6 seconds

Figure 1.3.   Federal Bureau of Investigation. "2015 Crime Clock Statistics." Photo in the public domain.

Weblink 1.4

To explore crimes known to the police, visit the FBI's *Uniform Crime Reporting* website: https://ucr.fbi.gov/. You can explore street crime, hate crime, human trafficking, and murders and assaults of law enforcement officers.

While our intent is not to undermine the extent and seriousness of crime, we cannot stress enough how deceptive, alarmist, and dangerous this reporting is. These are the numbers often used in the news and they tend to be further sensationalized with story lines such as "Murders, Shootings and Gun Sales per Day: An Average Day in United States."[28] Annually, you will be able to hear about the Crime Clock in televised news bringing alarming information into your homes. However, most of these stories do not put these numbers into perspective. They often omit the social and geographical context. For example, when considering that one murder occurs every 33.5 minutes, the journalists often do not tell us that this is more likely to occur in southern states and that victims are more likely to be young black males, who are often portrayed as violent criminals. As a result, people who are less likely to be victims of crime are left with an increased fear.

Police and Prosecutors in the United States

Media often portray policing as dangerous and liken it to a war zone. The Bureau of Labor consistently finds that government employees are substantially less likely than private sector employees to experience workplace violence involving a gun.[29] Yet, countless movies, television shows, and books entertain us with intense and frequent gun fights. In fact, Garcia (the first author of this book) loves to see a good crime movie that involves lots of crazy stunts, gun fights, and explosions. It is common for the media to present police as almost completely militarily trained, sharpshooters, and highly trained in forensics and criminal profiling. The truth of the matter is that most police personnel have never fired their gun in the line of duty (thankfully and for which most officers are thankful). Most police departments do not have the funds to provide the necessary training to enable police to become forensics and criminal profiling specialists. In fact, a forensics expert is required to have a science degree, typically a master's degree or a doctorate, while most criminal profile experts have psychology degrees. Examining police personnel, most have not completed a four-year college degree or even an associate degree (a two-year college degree).

When we examine the court process, research tells us that most cases sent to prosecutors are either dismissed or pleaded down to a lesser charge because there was not enough evidence to withstand the rules of evidence in a court of law or that prosecutors are only able to work with eyewitness testimony. In most cases, the eyewitness is the victim and it becomes a case of "he said-she said." Prosecutors are highly educated, having completed a four-year bachelor degree and a law degree. However, they are law enforcement personnel, not court officers, and tend to be overly concerned with high conviction rates and so try to negotiate guilty pleas. Most prosecutors do not take their cases to trial as you see in every episode of *Law & Order*.

Criminal Court Judges in the United States

Crime can be categorized as misdemeanors, which are less serious and often result in probation or jail time, or as felonies, which are more serious and can result in prison time. Fortunately, most crimes are misdemeanors and fall under the jurisdiction of a lower court. We typically know them as municipal court or town court among smaller populations. Across the nation, most small geographic locations fall under the jurisdiction of a town court that employs judges who do not have law degrees. In fact, many town court judges win elections based on popularity. As many judges have critiqued, there is no nationwide system of pre-judicial education.[30] Most of these programs do not result in a degree and the length of educational training is limited. In many of these cases, we find that the judges are making decisions outside of the law. This means that their decisions are not legal. Yet, judicial oversight is lacking and their decisions often go unquestioned.

Municipal and felony court judges are fully trained with law degrees and vast legal experience. The judge is an interpreter of the law. The judge is not supposed to have a personal opinion and discretion is decreasing every year. However, loopholes and a lack of oversight allow judges to bring politics into their decisions. Depending on the state, judges are either elected, in which case they want to show a record of convictions, or are appointed by the highest legislative figure of the state, the governor. So while the judge is supposed to be apolitical, the judge often becomes an advocate for the crime fighter. The judge tends to be tough on crime and often presumes that the defendant standing in the courtroom is guilty. Researchers have long found that the courtroom workgroup (i.e., the judge, prosecutor, and public defender) often work not toward obtaining the truth but toward sentence negotiation.

In her research, Venessa Garcia has witnessed judges engaging in sentence negotiation but she has also witnessed judges truly working to ensure due process of the law and recognizing defendant rights. It is a refreshing event to witness. However, news coverage rarely gives details of judicial decision-making unless it is a shocking decision or they gloss over these decisions. In movies and television, judges are often portrayed as umpires to a feuding prosecution and defense team. They often contain no substance.

The Defense Counsel in the United States

When we consider the defense side of the legal equation, we often do not find the high-paid criminal attorney likened to Johnnie Cochran nor do we often find the slimy ambulance chaser. Most defendants are working class or poor and must rely on overworked, underpaid public defenders or court-appointed attorneys who have no or little resources to investigate their clients' cases.[31] These defense attorneys are forced to rely solely on police evidence, which may have focused on their clients as the only possible suspect. The evidence may have been incomplete, improperly collected, or falsified. Public defenders, however, are expected to behave within the courtroom culture and advise their clients accordingly. This means that if they want the judge to rule favorably, they must avoid requesting continuances or objecting to statements made by the prosecution; in fact, they must try to convince the client to negotiate a guilty plea, thus avoiding a costly trial. Public defenders who insist on their client's day in court tend to find many road blocks in their job, and it is the subsequent client who pays for this lack of cooperation.

However, we have found many cases of incompetent defense attorneys. The Innocence Project started in 1992 by Barry Scheck and Peter Neufeld has been able to exonerate over 340 wrongfully convicted offenders.[32] Sixteen of the people they helped were convicted based on incompetent defense attorneys. Twelve of these innocent people had already served over fifteen years before they were exonerated.

Corrections in the United States

We do not know much about corrections officers and prison life. The United States houses 25 percent of the world's inmate population. We have imprisoned or jailed over 2.2 million offenders.[33] Even with two years of experience working with inmates in a maximum security prison, Garcia can state that prisons and jails are very mysterious places. It is hard even for researchers to fully examine how corrections officers do their jobs. Many inmates complain of abuse and torture, but unless we see immediate evidence of this abuse, as in the recent case of Rikers Island,[34] the public typically brushes these complains aside as lies told by hardened criminals. News media often only report about corrections officers when they engage in corruption or when a prisoner escapes. Movies and television shows tend to portray corrections officers as very corrupt and power hungry. Research shows that people tend to fall into this job instead having it as their childhood dream job, as you find with police. We also learn from research that corrections officers are trained to keep and not to correct. They are trained in security but their training lacks the necessary tools to help a population that often has emotional trauma and mental illness.

And we must not forget about the probation and parole officers[35] who supervise the vast majority of convicted offenders. We must not forget about them but the media does. They are often included as a side note in television shows and movies as someone who happened to be supervising the main character. They are rarely, if ever the main character. And one would be hard-pressed to find a news story on probation and parole. Yet, in 2014, there were 3,864,100 adults on probation and 856,900 adults on parole.[36] Probation and parole officers are hired to supervise offenders within the community. This involves helping them rehabilitate their behavior or addictions, develop work skills or find jobs, and care for their families. However, since the 1970s, the public no longer believes in rehabilitation[37] and so resources are hard to come by. In 2002, shortly after the authors first moved to New Jersey, Garcia was contacted by the New Jersey Parole Board, then a division of the New Jersey Department of Corrections, in order to write a grant for a community program that the government did not have. The main problem with corrections in the United States is that agencies do not understand the real reasons for criminal behavior and do not have the "know how" or the resources to help offenders. As a result, they reoffend (also known as recidivism). And we come full circle to discussing crime in the United States.

MORAL PANICS

Instead of taking the time to review research findings on crime and justice, our criminal justice system makes rash decisions based on uninformed public opinion. We say that it is uninformed because the public tend to obtain most of their "knowledge" from the media. This brings us full circle to our earlier discussion on media consumption. When we see a case of child rape, we cry for immediate conviction and policy change. The result is a law such as Megan's Law which has proven not to work and to be costly.[38] In fact, most child sex offenders are parents who are not covered under many sex offender registry laws. Research has found that in some states, when an offender is executed the violence in that state increases for the next six months. We also know through research that as much as 67 percent of youth who are locked up as part of their sentence will reoffend within twelve months. Yet, moral panics continue to drive policy and official decisions within criminal justice to lock away more people. We argue that media plays a large role in driving these moral panics.

CONCLUSION

This book examines the social constructs of crime and justice as they are portrayed by the media. Research has revealed that media depictions of crime and justice are not reflections of reality.[39] However, the public tends to use media depictions as their frame of reference. Furthermore, with the advent of social media, our "knowledge" of crime and justice in society has become ever more distorted. Our goal is to present these media depictions of crime and justice and compare them to the reality of crime and justice. Of specific importance is bringing to light how race, class, and gender play a role in crime and justice in reality and in the media.

This book adds significant information to the constructs held by the general public by placing media depictions into historical, legal, and social context. Media studies and criminology tend to be kept safe and secure within the walls of academia. Researchers write for other researchers, while the occasional college student (such as the second author of this book Samantha Arkerson) reads these works in order to complete term papers. It is our hope that we can bring to you the social science knowledge missed by media infotainment in a way that is enjoyable to read. Research findings as well as our own research will be shared without the complicated jargon. News media, crime movies, television crime dramas, and true crime television series will be discussed, keeping all of its fascinating coverage, while uncovering the reality of crime and justice. By the time you are done with this book, you will have a stronger appreciation of the realities of crime and justice. You will be in a better position to view crime news and true crime television series with a critical eye. And you will be able to view crime dramas as pure entertainment.

Chapter 2

News Media, Social Media, and Crime Waves

CRIME IN THE UNITED STATES

In this chapter, we discuss news media focus on violence and crime sprees. Research and government sources have long discovered that the most frequent crime type is property crime. However, researchers have noted that the media, most significantly news media, perpetuate the "violent predator" myth.[1] The violent predator myth is the belief that most crimes are violent street crimes that cost society the most lives and dollars. However, Welch, Fenwick, and Roberts found that while the annual cost of street crime amounts to approximately $4 billion, the annual cost of white collar crime amounts to $200 billion.[2] Furthermore, while in 1995, there were approximately 24,000 homicides, there were over 56,000 workplace deaths caused by unsafe working conditions. What people do not realize is that employers are required by federal law to ensure that the workplace is safe. However, even if employers knowingly maintain an unsafe work environment and are held accountable for these deaths, the government and society do not place them in the same category or seriousness as noncorporate homicide.

Most people rely on the media to gather their understanding of crime and justice. In fact, 96 percent of the average person's crime information is obtained from the media.[3] Ray Surette refers to this as symbolic reality.[4] He describes symbolic reality as all of the events, facts, and beliefs you hold as reality but never witnessed firsthand. By perpetuating the violent predator myth, the media help to construct the image of crime that becomes our symbolic reality. However, if this construction of crime omits the most deadly and costly crimes, what else does it omit. Media influence our fear of crime which in turn influences our beliefs of crime and punishment. But it is not that simple an explanation. Let us step back and examine how the media progressed into the crime business.

MEDIA AND EARLY CRIME NEWS

Crime news can be found after 1575 and was typically led by stories of murder, treason, and witchcraft.[5] In the United States, early crime news was printed in pamphlets and broadsides and often covered criminal trials of notorious crimes. The stories were often very brief and involved the most serious crimes. By the 1830s, broadsides were replaced by the penny press which printed stories that held more human interest. These stories relied on witnesses and were more critical of society and the justice system. For example, on October 11, 1851, *New-York Daily Times* released a story titled "Conviction for Arson—Exciting Developments."[6] The story opens describing that Mr. Henry T. Conklin was convicted of arson in the first degree, which was a much more serious crime at the time, and that it only took the jury eight minutes to deliver the verdict of death by hanging. Mr. Conklin was already under a "sentence of death" and was guilty of setting other fires. The news story described the trial as exciting and intense, witnessed by citizens who did not want the death penalty but who could not ignore the strong witness testimony. Mr. Conklin was named as the ringleader of a gang of arsonists who caused anxiety and property loss to the citizens of Utica, New York, in the winter of 1850. While details of the crime and trial were brief, the journalist linked the current crime to previous crimes and to the community and its sentiments.

As time passed, news reporting of crime changed to include graphic details as well as police accounts of the crimes. Neil Websdale and Alexander Alverez refer to this as *forensic journalism.*[7] As defined by Websdale and Alvarez, forensic journalism, similar to forensic science, gathers and reports minute details of the crime. However, unlike forensic science, forensic journalism does not rely on the scientific method. Instead, it follows a predetermined pattern of news reporting that relies on the accounts of police as gatekeepers and as agents of the state. Forensic journalism reports on the details, however gory, of the crime scene presenting police accounts as factual and only reporting on the immediate circumstances of the crime. In so doing, it focuses on individuals and individual crimes which necessarily overlook the larger social context of the crime, such as patterns of violence and their causes.

Websdale and Alvarez describe that forensic journalism can be described by three interrelated characteristics. First, forensic journalism is situationally based. For example, in the November 28, 1898 reporting of the death of Mr. and Mrs. Rhoner, the *New York Journal* reported the details of the crime scene in which Mr. and Mrs. Rhoner were found dead in their bed on a Sunday morning.[8] Continuing with the details, the story reports the Rhoner's ages, occupations, and typical Sunday morning routine. In order to demonstrate the details of the crime, the newspaper presented an illustration of the bedroom, top and side profile drawings of the Rhoners demonstrating the trajectory of the bullets, as well as rough portraits of Mr. and Mrs. Rhoner (see Figure 2.1). Nowhere in the story did the writer provide the social context of murder within New York nor did the writer provide who is typically found to be the culprit in this type of murder. Hence, there is no structural explanation of murder.

Second, Websdale and Alvarez describe the process of situationally based dramaturgical representations. By this, the researchers explain that the job of journalists, as if playing a role in a drama or a theater, is one in which police

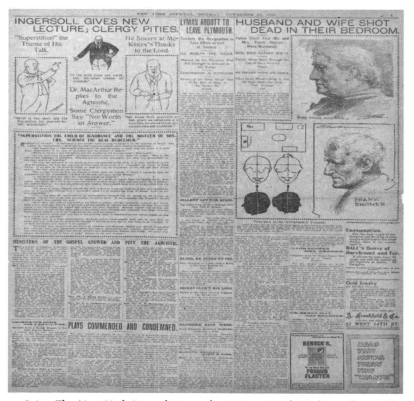

Figure 2.1. *The New York Journal*, **November 28, 1898. Photo from Library of Congress, Serial and Government Publications Division. Photo in the public domain.**

play the role of expert and official keeper of the facts while journalists play the role of the scientist. While Frank Rhoner, Jr., insisted that it was a case of murder–suicide, naming his father as the culprit, the reporter provided details given by the police as the more likely truth. The facts provided were that there were no powder marks found and that neither of the victims would have been able to shoot themselves in the top of the head as was the case at the scene.

The third characteristic of forensic journalism is internal myopia or near-sightedness. By maintaining internal myopia, the media do not engage in any reflection even on their own previous reporting of crimes. In the case of the deaths of the Rhoners, the reporter did not provide any comparisons to previous murders or murder–suicides. There was an alluding to expert knowledge of bullet trajectories and powder marks but no mention of similar cases in which such comparisons could be made. The deaths were reported in a silo with only a hint of questioning that tainted their surviving offspring.

Websdale and Alverez also tell us that forensic journalism does not demonize offenders. Instead they are tainted. As one reads the story of the Rhoners' deaths, Frank Rhoner, Jr., is described as reticent and uncooperative. Only by show of authority was the police officer able to gain entry into the home after the Rhoners were taken to the hospital where they died. However, the scene was cleaned of all evidence. Upon the son's insistence that it was a murder–suicide, the story claims that he could not provide proof of this claim. Even a letter given to him by his father that indicated how he should handle the property was not accepted as evidence to the claim. It was reported that Frank Rhoner, Jr., showed the letter to the coroner but refused to show it to the police. There was never a mention that the son was a likely suspect; however, the totality of the details reported tainted the twenty-four year old. The seemingly legitimacy of police as experts refutes any question of this tainting.

Yellow Journalism

About the same time that the Rhoner murders were published in the news, the nation saw the birth of yellow journalism. Yellow journalism was a style of news reporting that focused more on sensationalism and profits than it did on facts. It was with this style of reporting that journalists moved away from relying on court personnel and eyewitnesses and started to rely on the so-called expertise of the police. As history reveals, yellow journalism developed in the 1890s in a battle of reporting in order to dominate the New York newspaper market.[9] News publishers Joseph Pulitzer of the *New York World* and William Randolph Hearst of the *New York Journal* engaged in increasingly sensationalist-style reporting in order to increase their profits. The Spanish-American War is identified as the first media war in yellow journalism. Pulitzer and Hearst engaged in a battle of sensationalism in reporting on the atrocities experienced in Cuba at the hands of the Spanish. Though the media did not start the war, it had a strong influence in pulling the heartstrings of the American public and rallying support for the ensuing war.

Newspapers saw themselves as the police of society. In focusing on corruption they saw themselves as enforcers of the law. Although the *New York Journal* and the *New York World* were banned in certain libraries and reading rooms, such as the Newark Free Public Library, their form of news reporting was very successful and very profitable. Yellow journalism in its extreme did not last long. Before his death, Joseph Pulitzer became ashamed of his actions and brought his newspaper back to its former integrity. This move helped to end the era of yellow journalism; however, the damage was already done. Sensationalism, infotainment, and media competition drove what and how the news was reported.

Weblink 2.1

For a discussion of *U.S. Diplomacy and Yellow Journalism, 1895–1898*, go to: https://history.state.gov/milestones/1866-1898/yellow-journalism.

MAKING NEWS

The question becomes how do the media determine what will make the news. Ray Surette describes two competing models: the market model and the manipulative model. Each model is used to determine newsworthiness.[10] In the market model, public interest drives newsworthiness. Journalism under this model is respectable, objective, and reactive of the events. On the other hand, in the manipulative model, newsworthiness is determined by the needs and profits of the media organization. Under this model, news is sensational, reality is distorted, and news is proactive and used in swaying public opinion.

Surette argues that a third model is more realistic in describing newsworthiness: the organizational model. Surette argues that it is unrealistic to think that organizational factors do not drive news and that they can subjectively be eliminated from crime reporting. Aside from profits, criteria for the selection of newsworthy crime stories include seriousness of the crime, unusual circumstances, extraordinary events, involvement of high-profile people, and routinization. This can explain why murder is more frequently covered by the news media and why the violent predator myth persists. We also see stories of robberies of elderly (not a frequent crime), stories of bombings, serial killers and gang violence (while all are very serious, they are not nearly as frequent), and stories of the crimes of famous people.

Routinization, however, is very important. Journalists face organizational pressures to produce stories quickly, especially in the era of 24/7 news cycles. In order to achieve a quick turnaround of the news, reporters tend to follow a formula of reporting that is brief and to the point. Ray Surette describes the formula used for reporting crime.[11] First, the crime is announced, then the minute details are given, and finally, an account of police investigation is detailed. We can find this formula in crime reporting as early as the late 1800s and we can find it today. This requires journalists to focus on certain types of crimes (those mentioned earlier) that are nonroutine within society.

In order to keep the flow of crime reporting, journalists must then engage in an information-processing system. Within this system, the reporter develops close relationships with police, earning their trust and obtaining first-hand knowledge of crimes. On the other side, the police as the gatekeepers can determine what information is released and are able to frame the news perspective. Surette argues that this system creates a hierarchy in which the media are reporting on crimes against or of concern by those at the top of the hierarchy. These are the crimes of those at the bottom of the hierarchy. Meanwhile, news is reported to those in the middle of the hierarchy. In this way, most crime news focuses on the crimes of the poor and racial/ethnic minorities, even if they do not directly affect the white and wealthy masses. This keeps the focus on the individual, that is, street crime, and ignores crimes that cause widespread harm, that is, white-collar and government crime.

The seriousness of the crime, in addition to a concern for corporate profits, has led to an ideology of newsworthiness known as "if it bleeds, it leads." The origin of the term is unclear. Some claim that it was first used by journalist Eric Pooley in a 1989 *New York Magazine* article titled "Grins, Gore, and Videotape: The Trouble with Local TV News." In his article, Pooley claims that longer evening broadcasts are more likely to maintain some balance of news coverage. However, it is still riddled with sensationalism and "the well-written segment drowns in a sea of clichéd copy."[12] James Hamilton found that, by 1993, close to one-third of all local news stations in Miami, Florida, dealt with crime and one-third of those stories involved murder.[13] Hamilton stresses that this is problematic because high-crime stations target younger audiences whose media consumption is increasing. Using George Gerbner's *cultivation theory*, Hamilton points out that the longer people are exposed to the media the more likely they are to internalize the messages and themes provided within the media, the more they are to fear for their safety, and the more pessimistic they are about society. Hamilton claims that people who consume large amounts of violent media given in entertainment crime programming and news are more likely to develop the "mean world" syndrome.

Weblink 2.2

To learn more about cultivation theory, go to: https://masscommtheory. com/theory-overviews/cultivation-theory/.

TOWARD A 24/7 NEWS CYCLE

The amount of exposure to crime news was not as much of a concern in the recent past. One could turn on the morning news, the evening news (typically at six o'clock) and the nightly news (typically at eleven o'clock). Pre-cable television news could be found on network channels, that is, ABC, CBS, and NBC. Radio news could be gathered during commercials. One of oldest news radio stations, currently 1010 and owned by CBS, was once owned by William Randolph Hearst. 1010 radio became an all-news radio station in 1965 and boasts that it gives "All news all the time." This was a precursor to the *24/7 news cycle* which made news business even bigger business.

In the 1980s, the establishment of the first twenty-four-hour international news channel changed the face of news media. The Cable News Network, widely known as CNN, aired its first live broadcast on June 1, 1980, when it was reported that President Carter met with gunshot victim and civil rights activist Vernon Jordan and that a man experiencing a family problem engaged in a shooting spree on an Amtrak train injuring a passenger, a policeman, and the conductor.[14] CNN became so integral to crime reporting as well as international news reporting that scholars identified the *CNN effect*. The CNN effect is not unanimously accepted or consistently defined but the overall idea is that CNN with its constant presence internationally and its televised images forced government policy.[15] While media research debated whether the media transmit the news or make the news, the CNN effect supported the latter, known as the cultural model.[16] Regardless of the effect, CNN created a new form of news reporting known as the 24/7 news cycle. The 1010 radio's logo of "All news all the time" was now televised and created unprecedented competition in news reporting.

The 24/7 news cycles were further complicated when newspapers took to the internet in 1994. Nearly half of all newspapers could be found on the internet although the news was not updated more than once a day. The true meaning of 24/7 news cycles did not occur until the early 2000s when most newspapers could only be found online but were updated throughout the day.

Garcia subscribes to a local online news site, NJ.com, where she receives emails of new stories posted throughout the day. The use of the internet in crime reporting necessarily requires us to discuss social media.

SOCIAL MEDIA AND CRIME NEWS

As most people are aware, social media is the complex form of communication in which people and organizations use the World Wide Web to share information and create online communities. Social media can vary with time but as we write this book the most popular social networking sites are Facebook, Twitter, Instagram, SnapChat, YouTube, LinkedIn, Tumbler, Pinterest, and Reddit. Within social media communities, anyone can share important and not so important information any time of the day. When we consider the impact of social media on crime news reporting we have to understand how social media works. With the advent of 24/7 news cycles using the internet, traditional media become less of a creator of the news. News reporting is now on-demand news. On any social media platform, any person having read, viewed, or listened to a news story can repost the story and write comments on the issue. Because social media creates an online community, one posting or comment can snowball into a widely viewed news event.

Social media has influenced the news in many ways. Jeffrey Gottfried and Elisa Shearer, of the Pew Research Center found that 62 percent of U.S. adults obtain their news from social media.[17] In 2016, 66 percent of the adults who used Facebook obtained their news from that site.[18] We also learn that 70 percent of Reddit users and 59 percent of Tweeters obtain their news from those sites. Sharing news is a common activity on social media. Anderson and Caumont reported in 2014 that as much as 50 percent of social media users have shared or reposted news stories, images, or videos, while 46 percent of social media users discussed news events.[19] Your authors are notorious for doing this.

In this era of on-demand news reporting, the audience has been known for making news as well. As much as 14 percent of users post photos they took of a crime event and 12 percent post videos. You would be hard-pressed not to find personal videos of the protests and riots in Ferguson, Missouri, the Charlotte police protest, or the September 11 attacks (see Box 2.1 for other examples of the public making news).

Box 2.1.   Social Media Users Are Making the News

The use of social media to share news has been an ever-growing trend. As events unfold, witnesses to events frequently post videos and photos on YouTube or Facebook. However, social media have also added to growing evidence in criminal investigations. In December 2015, Kendra Beswick, aged twenty-four, was arrested after her husband posted video on Facebook in which he secretly recorded her abusing their children.[20] In October 2015, sixty-eight-year-old William Crum was charged with two counts of aggravated assault after a video that went viral caught him driving into a couple on a motorcycle, forcing them into a ditch (see Figure 2.2).[21] In September 2016, Baltimore police arrested Zanney Laws and Dakei Perry, both eighteen years old, for stabbing and robbing a sixty-four-year-old man. Evidently Zannery Laws recorded the crime on her cell phone and posted it on Facebook.[22] In November 2015, Nikey Dashone Walker and Shadeed Dontae Bey, both twenty years, robbed and beat a twenty-three-year-old man with cerebral palsy. The offenders recorded the crime with the victim's cell phone and then posted it on the victim's as well as their own Facebook pages.[23] More recently, the "Facebook Killer" posted his murder of seventy-four-year-old Robert Godwin on Facebook.[24] In each of these cases, not only did social media users give police evidence in which to build a case but their posting also lead news stories. While it is the media who determine which stories to pick up, the fact that they are getting their stories from their audience shows the level of input the audience has gained in helping to determine what is newsworthy.

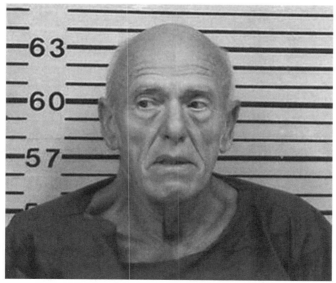

Figure 2.2. Mug shot of William Crum, 2015. Hood County Sheriff's Office. Photo in the public domain.

Finding news stories on social media often leads people to search for news on a particular topic or story instead of browsing through all of the news on a website as one would have done with a newspaper. People who visit a news site directly spend significantly more time on that site and browse more of the site's pages than do people who visit the site via a social media posting. Fifty-three percent of the people who use Facebook regularly see crime news. However, only 41 percent of Twitter users and 43 percent of Facebook users are willing to discuss news online. So while the audience is helping to shape the news, they still have a long way to go in determining newsworthiness.

Weblink 2.3

The Pew Research Center publishes a series called *Journalism and Media*. Visit this site at http://www.journalism.org/ to learn about the latest trends in how social media is affecting news media.

News media are well aware of the impact that the internet and social media have on news consumption. As a result, news reporting has shifted from broadcasting to narrowcasting. Narrowcasting is the process by which news media target smaller homogeneous audiences with their reporting. Highly focused news has been placed online. Whole websites and television channels have been devoted to particular interests uncovered by narrowcasting. To name a few, CNN, History Channel, Crime and Investigation Network, Discovery, MSNBC, and Investigation Discovery provide amateur crime solvers (i.e., the audience) with a fill of programming designed to reel in viewers.

When we examine traditional news media shows, we find obvious use of social media. For example, the *Today* show has incorporated the Orange Room into their daily programming. Carson Daly hosts this segment of the show sharing with viewers entertainment news and what the public has tweeted. Their website asks people to submit their photos, stories, views, and videos via such platforms as Twitter, Facebook, YouTube, Snapchat, and Instagram.[25] Major news stations have created social media websites. CNN provides a list of trending stories as well as a section known as "NewsPulse" that shows the most popular stories.[26] ABC, CBS, and NBC have all joined in the trend of using social media. While major news networks are acknowledging their desire to engage their audiences, the lack of focus on pressing social issues is a far cry from news.

In an attempt to give the audience more control over its news search, several social media news websites have been established. While some sites have a particular focus, for example, *Social Media Today*, *Bloomberg*, *Forbes*, and *Entrepreneur* all focus on business, our concern here is with social media news sites that allow you to search for crime and justice stories. Sites such as *Open Forum*, *CNN*, *The New York Times*, and *The Guardian*, to name a few, attempt to filter the news, blogs, and other online information on the web. Typically, news searches yield news stories, videos, press releases, speeches, testimony, podcasts, radio, and photographs.

Keeping abreast of the news tends to be seen as a younger person's activity. As discussed earlier, researcher James Hamilton found that news organizations try to reach younger audiences when reporting on the crime, so too does social media. *BuzzFeed* is a particularly popular website with younger audiences. Often when discussing crime in her classes, Garcia's students share stories that they read on *BuzzFeed*.

Fake News and Social Media

The latest issue with social media and news reporting is fake news. Fake news refers to false information that is made to appear as actual events in society and released by official-looking news sites. Fake news also includes political satire that makes light of or exaggerates facts within politics. With the ease of computer technology, it is not that hard to design a news story that appears official-looking. Furthermore, since over 60 percent of adults obtain their news from social media, these fake news stories, being posted and reposted to sites like Facebook and Twitter, go viral and take on a life of their own. Fake news is a growing concern of the media, law enforcement, and even politicians. Fake Twitter accounts have been found to release hoaxes. *The Rightists.com* sells itself as an "independent News platform That allow People and independent Journalist to bring the news directly to the readers" (written as shown on the website).[27] This declaration is followed by a statement that the site is a hybrid of news and satire. *The Denver Guardian* was a website designed specifically to provide fake news.

On November 9, 2016, *The New York Times* reported a fake news event that went viral.[28] Eric Tucker posted a tweet stating that anti-Trump protestors were bussed into Austin, Texas. With no proof, he included pictures of dozens of busses and claimed that the protests were fake, implying that the campaign was rigged. Within hours, conservative organizations reposted Tucker's tweet to Reddit, Facebook, and Twitter resulting in hundreds of thousands of links and shares. Even Donald Trump added to the fake news by tweeting that they were professional protestors who were incited by the media. After the facts were uncovered, Eric Tucker reposted his tweet with a note stating that it was false. However, this corrected tweet only received twenty-nine retweets and twenty-seven likes. Following this and other fake news, many have claimed that Hillary Clinton lost the 2016 presidential election because of social media.

One widely believed fake crime news told of an FBI agent responsible for uncovering Hillary Clinton's leaked emails who was found dead in his home along with his wife in a murder–suicide.[29] This fake news post showed a house fire that supposedly held the two bodies and resulted in 100 Facebook shares per minute. In a more damaging fake news story posted on Facebook, *The New Nationalist* and *The Vigilant Citizen* identified Comet Ping Pong pizzeria in Washington, D.C. as the location of a child-trafficking ring that was led by Hillary Clinton and John Podesta, her campaign chief.[30] This fake scandal was known as "PizzaGate." The results of this fake news were devastating. The restaurant owner and his employees received hundreds of death threats. Twenty-eight-year old Edgar Welch from North Carolina went as far as showing up to the restaurant with a .38 caliber revolver, searching the restaurant and firing several rounds into the restaurant. Fortunately, no one was hurt.

In a 2014 study, Meital Balmas found that the more people are exposed to fake news from political satire programs, the stronger are their feelings of inefficacy, alienation, and cynicism toward politicians.[31] Pushing forth the idea of media connectedness, Balmas found that people are unable to separate their experiences with hard news (real news) from their experiences with fake news. Indeed, Donald Trump consistently repeats "news" information that he has obtained from fake news sources. He also consistently calls news and news companies that he does not agree with fake news. Hard news and fake news interact and result in perceptions, attitudes, and behaviors. When news is perceived to be realistic, it has a greater impact. Hence, when we are bombarded with stories of violent predators and political conspiracies, it does not seem far-fetched that protestors would be bussed in to violently protest Donald Trump's run for presidency or that perhaps Hillary Clinton is so "crooked" that the whistle-blowing FBI agent would be so scared as to take his own life.

Research on fake news has predominantly focused on its effects on political events. We have yet to see research conducted on the effects of fake news on behavior such as crime and crime prevention. Anecdotal cases such as the PizzaGate shooter tell us that we need to examine this phenomenon more closely.

As a final note on fake news, if one doubts the impact of fake news, one has to simply consider the hysteria that followed the 1938 radio broadcast of Orson Welles's *The War of the Worlds*. Urban myth tells us that there was mass hysteria defined by millions of frightened people who took to the streets trying to flee an alien invasion.[32] The fact is that there were many people who, tuning in to the show late, did panic and attempt to flee for safety. However, as Brad Schwartz explains, the hysteria occurred on two counts: panic over an invasion and, more prominently, panic over the power of the media.

Weblink 2.4

To listen to NPR interview with Craig Silverman on the spread of fake news, visit: http://www.npr.org/2016/12/14/505547295/fake-news-expert-on-how-false-stories-spread-and-why-people-believe-them.

RACE, ETHNICITY, AND CLASS IN CRIME NEWS

The power of the media is especially important when they help to socially construct or reproduce images of criminals. Nowhere is this more important than when considering the stigmatization of minority groups. As we considered this topic, we contemplated where to place this discussion within the chapter. Assumptions of race, class, and gender permeate crime in the media. Our discussion of symbolic reality finds that society has defined a symbolic assailant as one who is black, male, and violent.[33] Often this criminal is viewed as a superpredator. Invariably, the criminal tends to be a minority in some fashion in race, ethnicity, income, or religion. As we watch the crime news on television or read about it, we are often shown stories of criminals who are black, poor, and male. Crime news on terrorism does not typically report on domestic terrorism which tends to be committed by white criminals. We are told that terrorists are Middle Eastern Muslims or Muslim Americans.[34] Otherwise, they are white or black Americans who have been radicalized by Muslim extremists. During the 2016 presidential election, it was common for Donald Trump to repeat the term "Muslim extremists." News stories looped Trump's claims that Muslims are terrorists and a threat to our society. Trump also made public claims that Mexican immigrants are criminals. In one famous speech, Trump stated,

> When Mexico sends its people, they're not sending their best. They're not sending you. They're not sending you. They're sending people that have lots of problems, and they're bringing those problems with us. They're bringing drugs. They're bringing crime. They're rapists. And some, I assume, are good people. (Written verbatim)[35]

The 2016 presidential election saw that Trump supporters were predominantly white, working class, males, with no college education, and were likely to believe such accusations about Mexicans and Muslims. The speeches he gave were riddled with fake news and became fake news therein.

One theory that can explain this phenomenon is called social identity theory. According to this theory, group membership is solidified and self-concept is strengthened by perceptions of those within one's group (i.e., the ingroup) as well as of those outside of one's group (i.e., outgroup).[36] The more importance a person places on the in-group, the more motivated is that person to protect the status of the group. Thus, members of the in-group are viewed in a more positive light and as complex. This is known as in-group heterogeneity. On the other hand, out-group members are more likely to be viewed in a negative light and as the same. This is known as out-group homogeneity.[37] Hence, white males were more likely to believe Donald Trump's tweets that he, a white male and unlike the many "unsuccessful" white and typically male politicians, can "Make America Great Again." At the same time, Trump's supporters believed that all terrorists are Muslim extremists, that all Muslims are a threat to America, and that all Mexican immigrants are criminals.

Kelsey Foreman and associates report that people with darker skin tones and facial features associated with African Americans were more likely to be viewed in a negative light by the media.[38] Additionally, black people are more likely to be represented in stories about poverty, homelessness, and public assistance. In 84 percent of crime stories involving black suspects, they are portrayed as violent, whereas 71 percent of crimes with white suspects are portrayed as violent. Blacks are also more likely to be depicted in stories about drugs, prisons, drug-addicted babies, AIDS, and suspects in police custody. As we see, race is equated with poverty and these are equated with crime. As a result, the hard news provided by legitimate sources as well as the fake news provided by illegitimate sources tend to cultivate the same messages.

Weblink 2.5

View YouTube video *Identity Theory vs. Social Identity Theory*, for a detailed discussion. Go to: https://www.youtube.com/watch?v=MUs_Y3z-I7c.

GENDER AND CRIME NEWS

When we consider gender, we do not find that minorities are more likely to be stereotyped as criminal. If this were the case then most crime stories would show women and girls as the majority of the criminals in our society. To the contrary, males are more likely to be portrayed as criminal. This ignores the fact that some criminal behavior of females has been increasing.[39] While arrests for males are five times higher than for females, female burglary and larceny-theft have increased in the past two decades.

Some crimes of females are completely overlooked in the media. When we read news stories of rape and sexual assault, the perpetrator is almost always a male, unless the victim is a minor. Sexual assault is the crime that young girls and women are socialized to fear the most. This is often referred to as the shadow of sexual assault.[40] In our fear, we assume that any crime can turn into a sexual assault. We are also taught to be weary of the stranger lurking in the shadows. This stranger, for many, is often a black male who will use any form of violence to rape a woman. Researchers call this the symbolic assailant. A Google search of rape on January 5, 2017, yielded over 10 million news stories. Reviewing the first several pages revealed one story of a female arrested for statutory rape (the victim was a minor) and one story of a female charged with kidnapping and intimidation in a rape committed by two men. Eighteen-year-old Myia Kilgore was charged with nonsexual assault crimes while her two male co conspirators were charged with rape and kidnapping.[41]

Official statistics show that females commit less than 1 percent of all forcible rapes.[42] This statistic has been constant for many years. In 2015, 409 females were arrested for rape, 85 involved female offenders under eighteen years of age.[43] When we do see female criminals in the media, they are often seen as committing crimes in collaboration with males. This is true for many crimes in reality.[44] As seen in the story of the kidnapping and intimidation charge against Myia Kilgore, official statistics show that females are often involved in forcible rapes involving multiple offenders (about 40 percent).[45]

Beyond sexual assault, the media have provided stories of infamous female violent predators. In the rare event of female serial killing, there was a media frenzy in the case of Eileen Wuornos. Between 1989 and 1991, Wuornos was a highway prostitute in California who shot, killed, and robbed seven of her Johns. Not only did the news media loop her trial and execution, but a blockbuster movie and a couple of documentaries also covered her life and crimes.[46] Adding to the news stories of infamous violent women were Susan Smith who drowned her two sons, Andrea Yates who drowned her five young children, and Rosemary West who, with her husband, raped, imprisoned, and murdered several girls and women, including her own daughter. Even less common is media coverage of women's property crimes. When women step too far out of society's gender role expectations, they are vilified. This was the case with Martha Stewart (see Box 2.2).

Box 2.2. Gendered Corporate Crimes: The Stories of Martha Stewart and Kenneth Lay

Martha Stewart is the most famous nonviolent female criminal of current times. Martha Stewart committed insider trading to the sum of $51,000.

She was convicted of conspiracy, obstructing justice, and giving false statement to federal investigators, and was sentenced to five months in prison followed by a two-year probation. Kenneth Lay, founder and chief executive officer of Enron committed securities fraud. Kenneth Lay cost his employees $2.07 billion in retirement and California customers $9 billion. Martha Stewart was a very wealthy and successful business woman and did not have the government connections that Kenneth Lay had. Lay's close government relations included President George W. Bush, Vice President Dick Cheney, and California governor Arnold Schwarzenegger. Although Lay was convicted, he died of a heart attack while on vacation in Colorado. This is freedom that a poor person would never be awarded.

Considering the enormous differences in the severity of Stewart's and Lay's crimes, one would think that Lay and the Enron scandal would overtake media coverage. After all, Enron and three other major corporate crimes cost the U.S. economy a loss of $7 trillion. Between November 2001 and July 2002, chapter 11 bankruptcy protection was criminally filed by Enron ($63.3 billion), Global Crossing ($25.5 billion), Adelphia ($24.4 billion), and Worldcom ($107 billion).[47] These crimes were all led by white wealthy male corporate executives. This compares to Martha Stewart's $51,000 insider trading crime.

In a study of these two cases alone, Carol Stabile found that within *The New York Times* (the crimes and corporations were largely located in New York) Martha Stewart's crime was covered by 1,279 news stories, while Kenneth Lay's crimes were covered by 23 news stories.[48] Martha Stewart's case was also covered in various news sections, such as general news, home, business, lifestyles, and sports. On the other hand, stories on Kenneth Lay and the other corporate criminals tended to be relegated only to the business sections. Further, while Martha Stewart was also covered by the tabloids, Kenneth Lay was not. Perhaps Kenneth Lay's political connections kept him out of the limelight and Martha Stewart's public relations staff (reputation managers)[49] kept her in the limelight. However, researchers have long found that in American popular culture, wealthy women have often been vilified if they stepped too far away from gender norms. In the case of Martha Stewart, she was rich and powerful and

> powerful women do not conform to subservient and heteronormative models of female behavior (who do not in some way demonstrate or act out their subservience) are simply not tolerated for long (if at all) within

the highest levels of private or public institutions. (parentheses included in original quote)[50]

If youth today were to search the newspapers, they would most likely believe that Martha Stewart was one of the worst criminals but not know much about Kenneth Lay.

CONCLUSION

Without a doubt, news media provides symbolic reality to its audience. News media influences the public's perception and behavior. However, we still have yet to discover the extent of this influence. How many Edgar Welch's are there who are willing to act out violently in response to fake news? Research tells us that most people are not swayed toward violence as a result of their media consumption. However, we must still explain the few that are. And while we have moved away from yellow journalism, many question how far we have actually moved. We still find sensationalism in the news. And with the spreading of fake news, many are willing to believe things such as PizzaGate and that all Mexicans and Muslims are a threat. The advent of social media makes the impact of crime news more significant. It is often difficult to determine what is real and what is fake. Add to this the symbolic reality of minorities within crime news, we do not truly get the big picture. What we do know is that news media sways public opinion and public opinion sways government policy. That is more than enough to further examine this form of media.

Chapter 3

Framing and Narrating Crime in the News

FRAMING CRIME

Regardless of the form of dissemination, news media must determine how they will compose their stories. In addition to looping and infotainment, media tend to create *frames* when addressing crime and justice. Ray Surette, one of the most well-known criminologists in the field of crime and media, wrote that "prepackaged constructions, or frames, include factual and inter-pretative claims and associated policies."[1] Media framing allows consumers to absorb an organized experience of crime and justice that is neatly categorized and labeled and quickly learned in the same way as is done in the process of socially constructing reality. Additionally, these frames are a reflection of what is believed within the larger society. Thus, the media are also part of the social construction process.

Through media framing, we become familiar with stories about school shooters, police heroes, and terrorists. For example, a recent study conducted by Aysel Morin examined the framing of terror versus crime in newspaper reporting of two widely covered shootings on military bases located on American soil.[2] We learned that news frames reflect the common sentiment that all crimes involving Muslims are viewed as terrorism. Morin's examination of the terror and crime frames not only represents society's sentiments but it also reinforces it. We also learn from the media research in criminology that due to the newness of this area of study definitive frames are not yet agreed upon.

In addition to crime frames found in the news, we obtain more details with narratives. Ray Surette explained that "narratives outline the recurring crime-and-justice types and situations that regularly appear in the media."[3] We are comfortable with the narratives provided. They tell the story within the frame and describe the characteristics of the criminals, victims, witnesses, and justice officials involved. Within a school shooter frame, a typical narrative tells us that these shooters tend to be disgruntled men who have a history of mental illness, such as Adam Lanza, the Sandy Hook shooter.[4] The problem with narratives is that they do not tell us of other possible narratives since the media tend to follow formulas. As a result, we are exposed to what is believed to be the typical offender. In a racist society, both past and present, this results in creating a symbolic assailant, as discussed in Chapter 2 and further elaborated later. So what are these frames and their accompanying narratives? We introduce media frames here and go into more detail in Chapter 4 in our discussion of crime in the movies.

MEDIA FRAMES WITHIN THE NEWS

Media researchers have identified episodic frames that focus on the crime event solely and thematic frames that link stories under a common theme. While news media are more likely to use episodic frames, we will also examine thematic frames that are commonly found within news media frames. Media researchers have uncovered various frames within news storytelling. Theodore Sasson uncovered cultural frames of street crime that are widely accepted today.[5] According to Sasson, there are five common frames the media use in discussing street crime within the news: the faulty system, blocked opportunities, social breakdown, racist system, and violent media. However, since the events of 9/11, U.S. society has placed more focus on terrorism. As a result, we pull the war on terror theme from the faulty system frame placing it as its own frame, known as the war on terror frame. Each frame provides an explanation for crime, telling us who is responsible and why, and provides an argument for the necessary crime control policy.

The Faulty System

The faulty system frame portrays crime as resulting from the inability of the criminal justice system to apprehend and punish criminals. This frame has its roots in classical criminology and rational choice theory. Consequently, people are free-willed thinkers who rationalize the benefits and the costs of committing a crime. If the punishments are swift, severe, and certain, then people will be deterred from committing crime. However, if the system is faulty then deterrence cannot be achieved. The 1970s and 1980s were rife with this theme as we were besieged with police corruption and Supreme Court decisions favoring offenders' due process rights. In the 1990s, the

O. J. Simpson case was often presented using this frame. Within the entertainment media or the news (infotainment media), the narrative portrayed the criminal justice system as incapable of helping innocent people within society. This is seen in narrations of police inability to make a solid arrest or, in the case of O. J. Simpson, in the prosecution's inability to battle Simpson's Dream Team. It is also seen in Judge Ito's inability to tame the media within his courtroom (see Box 1.1 in Chapter 1).

Sasson argued that smaller themes can be found within the faulty system frame.[6] These smaller themes can also be referred to as narratives, that is, they provide the details of the frame or the story. The "revolving door justice" theme shows the courts as too lenient in punishment, too slow, or too liberal. We see this revolving door justice theme in the case of Brock Turner (discussed later), who was sentenced to three months for sexually assaulting an intoxicated and unconscious young woman.[7] The assumption is that he will do it again. Public sentiments that the criminal justice system is too lenient in this case lead to protests and calls for removal of the sentencing judge.

The second theme, "adult crimes, kiddy punishments," claims that juveniles are committing serious crimes but receiving lenient sentences. The 1993 murder of a four-year-old boy by thirteen-year-old Eric Smith in Savona, New York, shocked the public with the gruesome nature of the killing and the subsequent nine-year sentence.[8] Six years later, twelve-year-old Lionel Tate was sentenced to life in prison without the possibility of parole after killing a six-year-old girl while imitating wrestling maneuvers on her. Five years after his conviction, Tate's sentence was overturned based on his immature mental capacity. He pleaded guilty to second-degree murder and was given a ten-year probation sentence.[9]

If you were to conduct a Google news search of the term "youth violence," you would find over 31,500 stories. A Google news search of school shootings in the United States yields over 119,000 news stories. News stories of school shooters often focus on the failure of the government to enact stricter gun control laws, which has been a concern in the past few years. Keep in mind that many of these stories are the product of looping, but each one adds to the strength of the frame.

Sasson's third theme claims that the faulty system can be defined by the construction of "luxury prisons" where inmates are coddled and given luxuries that even law-abiding citizens do not receive. Today's news, over a decade after Sasson published his work, does not engage in much prison conversation. Stories that cover corrections officer corruption, mentally ill inmates, unconstitutional crowding, beatings of inmates, and prison breaks are more common than stories of escaped convicts and luxury prisons. We have seen a move to a frame of *corrupt and inhumane prisons and jails* in an era when mass incarceration is seen as a problem to a functional society and successful prisoner reentry (i.e., the move from prison to society) is an increasing focus.

The "handcuffed police" theme presents police as being tied down by senseless rules that give criminals undeserved rights and denies justice to victims. In our war on terror, police have been faced with demands to quickly apprehend terrorists but are criticized for randomly stopping suspicious people. In New York City, news reports revealed that stop-and-frisk came under attack as a sanctioned policy of racial profiling.[10] A Google news search for stop-and-frisk stories for New York City alone yields over 37,000 stories. In 2013, stop-and-frisk was a major topic in the mayoral election and received a lot of media attention. Also in 2013, the federal court ruled that New York City's stop-and-frisk was discriminatory and unconstitutional. However, during the 2016 presidential election Donald Trump, not knowing that New York City's policy was declared unconstitutional, praised its practice. Since then the media have increased their focus on this topic.

Sasson also identified the "officer friendly" theme when discussing police. He found that people believe that police are most effective when they "walk the beat" instead of remaining nameless within a patrol car. Today, in the face of police shootings and national criticism of racist police, you find few news stories of police good deeds. News stories report on police dancing with youth and helping motorists on hot days. However, many of these stories do not make national headlines unless they go viral on social media. A recent story to go viral was a case in which Yukon, Oklahoma, police officers surprised an autistic boy on his birthday after receiving a call from an unknown individual stating that no one may show to the party.[11]

Sasson labeled the final theme within this frame "just pay the Edison bill" (Edison was the Boston power company). In this theme, culture holds to the belief that the death penalty is more effective and cheaper than a lengthy incarceration. Today, this is not a topic well covered in the news as the country moves further away from the practice of capital punishment. Currently, twenty states have abolished capital punishment. The country is at an all-time low on capital sentences as well as executions since the early 1990s.[12] In 2016, there were 2,905 inmates on death row in the nation but only twenty-seven new capital sentences were given that year. New capital sentences have declined 56 percent since 2012. Executions are at its lowest since 1992. One can find many stories of criminals receiving capital punishment. However, looping is responsible for many stories since new sentences are now rare. What is common is to find many stories about the morality and constitutionality of using the death penalty. Typical news stories center around legislative debate. When the news story centers around a violent criminal sentenced to death, the ultimate message is that some people need to be executed for their crimes.

Weblink 3.1

For research on the practice of stop-and-frisk in New York City, visit the Vera Institute: https://www.vera.org/publications/coming-of-age-with-stop-and-frisk-experiences-self-perceptions-and-public-safety-imp lications?gclid=CjwKEAiA2OzDBRCdqIyIqYaaqQoSJABeJZdiPMTC Se7iURNcjn3boU-Wx2PWoy5Jiq_q7AiKQ1ZIYBoCEbzw_wcB.

Blocked Opportunities

The blocked opportunities frame shows that crime is the product of poverty and inequality. This frame has a marked similarity to Robert Merton's strain theory.[13] Accordingly, the image of the criminal is an innovator who finds new yet-illegitimate ways of gaining wealth. Furthermore, as Sasson pointed out, blocked people are clearly able to see what they do not have through media images. Even with some gains, they often remain in the same homes and neighborhoods believing that there is another world they will never access. However, we can extend the idea of blocked wealth to other goals such as being blocked from power, as we find in many movies, or blocked from a desired job, educational goal, or a relationship.

When crime results from nonmonetary strain, we may apply Robert Agnew's general strain theory.[14] According to Agnew, people who experience various forms of strain and who have weak coping mechanisms are more likely to engage in crime. Strain, then, can involve being blocked from obtaining a positively valued goal, such as money, a job, or a grade. A second form of strain can involve having a negative situation imposed upon a person; for example, experiencing a violent victimization or having a boss behave hostilely. The third strain that Robert Agnew identified involves the removal of something valued in one's life. Agnew claimed that this last strain results in the greatest frustration. Additionally, the more people believe that the strain was received in an unjust and unfair manner, the more likely they are to become angry and act out with crime. In these cases, crime may serve as revenge. Media have no shortage of examples of blocked opportunities in the news, on television, or in the movies. While the crime news may make references to poverty and inequalities, these social problems are not commonly referred to as the predominant causes of crime. Instead, the social breakdown frame, discussed next, is given more attention.

Crimes most likely to result from economic strain are those in which money is quickly obtained: robbery, burglary, bank robbery, motor vehicle theft, and drug trafficking. Most crime news stories use forensic journalism providing situationally based facts of the event, maintaining internal myopia.

Furthermore, the need to produce stories quickly in the current age of the 24/7 news cycle, routinization, and the use of formulas increases. This results in providing brief details about the situation but not much about the criminal. Stories that provide the blocked opportunities frame tend to link crime to poverty and unemployment, at least in part, but do not add a human factor.[15] They often tell the audience about conditions in society and policies that work or do not work.

Reporting on revenge crimes has increased with the advent of revenge porn. A Google news search of revenge porn yields 1.4 million hits. Revenge porn is the act of posting or texting in social media or a cell phone sexually graphic images of another person without consent in a fit of anger. Victims tend to be female and in many cases the crime is a form of continued victimization in cases of intimate partner violence or rape. Typical news stories refer to jilted lovers and "dumped" boyfriends. Unlike most crime reporting, the media often focus on the damage that revenge porn does to the victim. In one *New York Post* report, the journalist described the damage to the victim's life, being unable to obtain a job or even an internship.[16] Because revenge porn is a new phenomenon, the media have also placed a lot attention on legislative changes.

Revenge killing is another crime type in which the media have applied the blocked opportunities frame. In these cases, the offender perceives an unjust wrongdoing against himself or herself and acts out violently. A recent case is the revenge killing of four people in Omaha, Nebraska.[17] In this case, a former doctor, Anthony Garcia, killed an eleven-year-old boy and the fifty-seven-year-old housekeeper of Dr. Hunter in 2008. In 2013, Anthony Garcia then killed pathologist Roger Brumback and his wife. Anthony Garcia killed all of his victims by slashing them with a knife. According to the news, Anthony Garcia blamed Drs. Hunter and Brumback for telling medical schools that he was fired, thus preventing him from obtaining another job.

Weblink 3.2

To learn more about federal and state revenge pornography laws, visit Cyber Civil Rights Initiative: https://www.cybercivilrights.org/revenge-porn-laws/.

Social Breakdown

The social breakdown frame presents crime as the result of broken families and communities. This frame follows a theory in criminology known as social disorganization theory. As is found in criminological research, some crime is related to the breakdown of traditional values (i.e., respect for authority, elders, and the family; decline of religion; and decline of personal responsibility), the family (i.e., divorce, teen pregnancy, parental neglect, and family violence), and the community (i.e., not knowing your neighbors). The social construction of crime within this frame follows a conservative ideology or a liberal ideology.

The conservative ideology argues that the social breakdown is a result of cultural deficiencies. This means that society believes that the culture in question lacks the ability to hold the family and community together. In short, they are morally deficient. In a human interest piece published in *The New Yorker*, journalist Rachel Aviv narrates a story about a young man, Rodricus Crawford, who was sentenced to death for the murder of his toddler son. While Aviv focuses on injustice done to Crawford, with evidence of a shoddy autopsy and hints of a racist prosecutor, she also presents the prosecutor's frame of a young black man who spends his days smoking marijuana instead of getting a job. In the news story, the journalist clearly shows the prosecutor framing the man's life with the breakdown of traditional and family values. Crawford would not work and his mother and other family members allowed him to smoke marijuana all day, not seeing it as a problem. It must be noted that today most sociologists and criminologists recognize this ideology as highly racist.

The conservative ideology is much more commonly used than the liberal ideology, which argues that social breakdown occurs as a result of blocked opportunities. In 2016, the City of Chicago experienced record high gun violence. Media coverage showed Donald Trump calling for the use of stop-and-frisk in Chicago, although declared unconstitutional in New York. In a *PBS NewsHour* article, Megan Thielking reported on social research conducted by Harvard and Yale professors that approaches crime as a social disease.[18] In this social disease, the researchers argue, those who socialize with criminals are much more likely to be victims of gun violence. They argue that gun-prevention policy should be victim focused and not offender focused. This argument falls under the conservative ideology and focuses on social networks on an individual level that then spreads. This is the more common media narrative of the social breakdown.

Thielking, however, compares this to Dr. Branas's research, of the University of Pennsylvania, who argues that prevention policy also needs to focus on hot spots and not just "hot people." This argument utilizes the liberal ideology and focuses on neighborhoods, their breakdown, and the lack of education and employment. Looking at news stories on crime as a social disease, we are much more likely to find the focus on the conservative ideology. In reporting the crime news with this framing, the media go only slightly beyond the situationally based facts of crime but do not address the structural causes of crime. Hence, the consumer is not given the bigger picture.

Weblink 3.3

For a closer look at strain and structural theories of crime, visit *Sociology of Deviance and Crime* at ThoughtCo: http://sociology.about.com/od/Disciplines/a/Sociology-Of-Deviance-Crime.htm.

Racist System

The racist system frame describes that crime is a result of the discrimination found within the criminal justice system. This frame has its roots in labeling and conflict theories. Here the question is not why do minorities commit crime but why are the police, courts, and corrections preoccupied with the crimes of minorities? The frame puts more focus on police racial profiling and racially motivated violence. According to labeling theorists, the act does not make one a criminal. Instead, it is society's reaction to the person who commits the crime that makes him or her a criminal. Thus, an individual could engage in sexual assault and not be labeled a deviant or criminal because of her or his race or her or his power.

In Box 3.1, we compare two sexual assaults, one committed by a white college student Brock Turner and the other committed by a black student Corey Batey. Turner was sentenced to a few months in jail, while Batey was sentenced to fifteen years in prison. Labeling theorists would claim that because Turner was given such a lenient sentence, he was labeled as less criminal, while Batey's fifteen-year sentence labels him as a very dangerous predator. In a racist system frame, the black person is the target of racism in this labeling process.

Conflict theory is the larger theoretical framework in which labeling theory resides. According to conflict theorists, people in power make, interpret, and enforce the laws in order to ensure that they keep their power. This necessarily keeps those who are not in power powerless. This theory was developed by Karl Marx in order to explain economic inequalities; however, in the 1970s, conflict theorists added race to this equation. Hence, according to the theory, we find that the poor and racial and ethnic minorities are systematically kept out of power. These theorists would claim that Turner was seen as a less-threatening individual due to the color of his skin and that is why his sentence was so light.

Recent news stories that use the racist system frame can be found among those that support the Black Lives Matter movement. Recent police shootings of such black men as Walter Scott, Terence Crutcher, and Keith Lamont Scott tend to be reported using separate media frames. In one media frame, police shot an innocent victim because he was black. Media frames most commonly start with the racist system frame but as the story unfolds, they often quickly move to the social breakdown frame. The story often ends with the narrative that the police shot and killed a criminal who exists within a socially broken neighborhood or culture. Within the racist system frame, the police shoot because they see black men as dangerous. These actions reinforce the notion of the symbolic assailant.

The symbolic assailant, again, is the person who society, as a whole, defines as the offender. According to Stacy Mallicoat and Connie Ireland, the symbolic assailant is seen as the minority male who lurks in the shadows awaiting the innocent victim.[19] In most cases, when the symbolic assailant is discussed among researchers, it is in reference to sexual assault and murder. The victims of these assailants are defined as innocent, unsuspecting, and unprovoking. Hence, when we come across news stories of rape, we often read about a black man stalking an innocent woman at night. Because symbolic assailants become part of our social constructs of crime and criminals, when we come across cases that do not follow this script, they are not defined to be as dangerous as the symbolic assailant and symbolic crime. This furthers the argument that the system is racist.

The symbolic assailant is typically examined in the research on sexual assault. The historical and current practice has been to provide the characteristics of the sex offender who violently rapes an innocent woman. This narrative paints the offender as a black male who is violent, predatory, and stalks unsuspecting usually white women who do everything right to live a good life (i.e., the innocent victim). In this narrative, the victim is *doing gender*. This means that she behaves like a good woman. She may have a job or be in school but her ultimate goal is to meet a good man, get married, and have 2.3 children. She does not engage in excessive partying behavior, if at all, and she does not date too much. She is most definitely not promiscuous.

The Central Park Jogger was such a victim. On April 19, 1989, twenty-eight-year-old Trisha Meili was raped and beaten while jogging in Central Park. The media described her attackers as a gang of young male black and Hispanic teens. The media also described Trisha Meili as a health conscious, hardworking investment banker.[20] In the end, the one Hispanic and four black teenagers were convicted with sentences ranging from five to fifteen years. The unfortunate circumstance is that in the rush to convict these symbolic assailants, the wrong people were convicted. In 2002, Matias Reyes, a male Hispanic teenager at the time, confessed to the violent attack. DNA evidence supported his confession.

Research has consistently found that rapists are not treated as harshly as other violent offenders. Furthermore, when the crime does not follow the narrative or the definition mandated by the symbolic assailant or when the victim does not play her role, then we tend to question the validity of her claim. In 2003, the media printed headlines of a rape accuser as "nutty or slutty" in the rape case against famous basketball star Kobe Bryant.[21] In this case, the victim was found to have had sex with another man after the rape was alleged to have occurred. The media even focused on the fact that the victim wore purple G-string underwear the day of the alleged rape. These are not behaviors that society accepts of a decent woman. Furthermore, these rape myths claim that only decent women can be raped—because bad girls never say "no." After a barrage of media attacks to her character, the victim dropped the charges.

Weblink 3.4

For a discussion of *Sexual Violence Myths and Facts*, visit Rape Victim Advocates: http://www.rapevictimadvocates.org/what-you-need-to-know/myths-and-facts/.

Box 3.1.   The Symbolic Assailant and Sexual Assault

In recent news, Stanford University student and member of the swim team Brock Turner, aged nineteen, was sentenced to three months in jail (a secure facility where less-serious offenders are incarcerated, as opposed to prison).[22] On January 18, 2015, two international Stanford University students came upon Brock Turner as he was sexually assaulting an intoxicated and unconscious young woman of twenty-two years. After the students chased and restrained him, Brock Turner was arrested, tried, and convicted. While the prosecution argued for a longer sentence, Judge Aaron Perskey only sentenced him to three months in jail. In his statement Judge Perskey stated,

> I think you have to take the whole picture in terms of what impact imprisonment has on a specific individual's life. And the impact statements that have been—or the, really, character letters that have been submitted, do show a huge collateral consequence for Mr. Turner based on the conviction.[23]

It was the character letter submitted to Judge Perskey by Brock Turner's father that had the greatest influence on the sentence.[24] Mr. Turner described his son as hardworking and having potential. In a rare media report, the Brock Turner case was placed into the larger social context. Zeba Blay wrote that the "rape culture and 'race' culture intersect."[25]

She explains that "potential" is equated with whiteness from which black men cannot benefit.

At around the same time, Vanderbilt University student and football player Corey Batey, aged nineteen, was also arrested and tried for raping an unconscious woman.[26] In both cases, the offenders were college athletes, were intoxicated during the assault, and had ample evidence to the crime. Batey was tried, convicted, and was given a fifteen-year prison sentence. In the aftermath of Batey's sentence, social and news media decried the racial injustice that seems apparent in these two cases (see the King story cited earlier). On one side of the equation, Turner was treated more as a victim of the system than an offender and his sentence did not reflect what was mandated by the law and past practice. On the other side of the equation, most news stories do not belabor the fact that Turner committed a sexual assault, not a rape, acted alone, and used his finger only (which is bad enough!), while Batey engaged in a gang rape with three of his teammates. Additionally, Batey and his fellow rapists urinated on the unconscious young woman, called out racial slurs while repeatedly raping her, and then dumped her unconscious body in an alley. They videotaped their crimes.

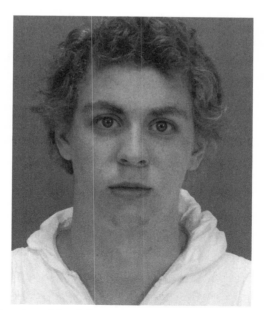

Figure 3.1. Mug shot of Brock Turner, 2015. Santa Clara County Sheriff's Office. Photo in the public domain.

The cases of Brock Turner and Corey Batey differ in many ways. However, protestors and the media claim that the only relevant difference is their race. Journalists such as Zeba Blay claim that it is the race and rape culture that allows for this discrimination to persist. Blay argues that black men who rape should not be absolved of their crimes but that white men should be held to the same standard. For a culture that holds so strongly to the symbolic assailant, a country with media who perpetuate this narrative in most of its crime stories, this outcome is, unfortunately, no surprise.

Figure 3.2.   Mug shot of Cory Batey, 2013. Metro Nashville Police Department. Photo in the public domain.

Violent Media

In the violent media frame, crime is learned after watching violent movies or playing violent video games. This frame relies on social learning theories. Cultivation theory, as discussed earlier, shows how people internalize what they learn from the media. The more negative exposure, the more negative their attitudes. There are several widely accepted learning theories. However, the one that is most frequently used when linking violent media to violent behavior is Bandura's modeling theory. In 1963, Albert Bandura, Dorothea Ross, and Sheila Ross published a famous study that examined the imitative aggressive behavior of young children.[27] This study exposed ninety-six young boys and girls to violent and nonviolent films, cartoons, and real behavior. After the children viewed the behavior, they were given toys, including a five-foot inflated Bobo doll. What the researchers found was that after viewing human and cartoon models of aggression on film, children were twice as likely to be aggressive. This study, famously referred to as the "Bobo doll study" by students of psychology and criminology, concluded that aggressive behavior is modeled, or imitated, as a result of exposure to violent media. Although, Albert Bandura later found this relationship to be much more complex,[28] many people in society tend to hold to this simplistic view.

While the research has yet to make the direct connection between violent media exposure and violent behavior, we still see some violent media frames in the news. We would remind you that media frames are social constructions that may or may not be grounded in reality but that are strongly believed to be fact among members of society. Nevertheless, some recent news coverage has pointed to research that found that exposure to violent video games decreases real-life violence because the gamer is given an outlet for aggression.[29] Some news outlets, however, print stories in order to sell products. This particular story was accompanied by announcements of video game releases. In a similar focus, another online news source reported that the American Psychological Association found that violent gaming increases aggression.[30]

In 2015, the *Daily News* released a story of a twenty-year-old man, Brandon Hoffman, who killed his girlfriend's eighteen-month son in a botched attempt to demonstrate a WWE wrestling maneuver.[31] Many years earlier, Lionel Tate, discussed previously, was given a life sentence for the murder of a six-year-old girl that he killed while imitating wrestling maneuvers. In these crimes, the media reported that the deaths were a result more of imitation than nefarious motives. In the 1980s and 1990s, the media reported on the growing concern that gangster rap music incites hostility toward law enforcement, misogyny, gang activity, and violence. In 1999, teenagers Eric Harris and Dylan Klebold shot and killed thirteen people and wounded twenty more in Columbine High School.[32] In the media looping of this horrific event, there were lots of stories and rumors that the teens were part of the "Trench Coat Mafia," now assumed to be false, that they were imitating the movie *The Matrix*, and that they aspired to outdo the Oklahoma City bombing.[33] The case resulted in a media frenzy to report on other similar crimes and discuss why school violence occurs.

Weblink 3.5

Review some of the conflicting research findings on violent media at Psychology: Science in Action: http://www.apa.org/action/resources/research-in-action/protect.aspx.

The War on Terror

The war on terror frame has been a commonly used frame in the media as of late. However, terrorism as a media frame has been used throughout history. In fact, the media and many political researchers call the 1970s the "golden age of terrorism."[34] Bombings in the United States were not uncommon, compared to about two dozen terrorist attacks since 9/11. In the 1970s, 184 people were killed and hundreds more injured due to many terrorist attacks. After the tragic loss of human life on September 11, 2001, seventy-four people have been killed due to terrorist attacks in the United States. However, the terrorism frame has changed since the 1970s.

In the 1970s, some terrorist groups included Weather Underground (forty-five bombings), Black Panthers (twenty-four bombings), and Fuerzas Armadas de Liberacion Nacional Puertorriquena (eighty-two bombings). While there were terrorist attacks by non-U.S. citizens, such as Palestinian terrorists and Croatian nationalists, most of the terrorists of the 1970s were domestic. Terrorist groups fought for such causes as ending the Vietnam War, fighting for and against civil rights,[35] and the liberation of Puerto Rico.

Since the attacks of 9/11, the terrorism frame has been altered a bit. Today, the United States' primary focus are jihadist terrorists from the Middle East. After the attacks of 9/11, President George W. Bush declared war on terrorism. This war on terror frame became popular six years after Sasson's 1995 book was published. Sasson would probably argue that this frame is embedded within the faulty system. In our war on terror, police have been faced with demands to quickly apprehend terrorists but have their hands tied with "pesky" rules such as the Fourth and Eighth Amendments. Garcia and Arkerson do not see these extremely important constitutional rights as pesky; however, many within society and the criminal justice system do.

Unlike most crime reporting, the news media tend to use a thematic frame.[36] Non-terrorist crime stories tend to be reported using episodic frames focusing on situationally based details of the crime event. Whenever there is a mass shooting or an attempted bombing, however, the news media typically question if the attacker has Muslim and Islamic ties. This reporting tries to link the offender with existing terrorist groups, namely ISIS. The war on terror media frame focuses, on one end, on the conservative ideology within the social breakdown frame. They typically report on the attacker's feelings of alienation, family conflict, and mental instability. For example, Tashfeen Malik, one of the December 5, 2015, San Bernardino terrorist attackers, was described as increasingly isolated and increasingly religious.[37] Zale H. Thompson was described as a recent Islamic converter and self-radicalized man who attacked a New York City police officer with a hatchet on December 2, 2015. Thompson was also described as unemployed and "a depressed recluse."[38] One would be hard-pressed to find any other type of media framing with terrorists.

In the early days of the war on terrorism, the faulty system was commonly used. The media frequently reported on the inability of the police to easily investigate suspicious people. Early into the war on terrorism, President Bush passed the PATRIOT Act.[39] During the construction of the Act, news media reported on public fears and demands for protection. In covering the ensuing opposition to what was perceived to be an acceptable infringement on the privacy and civil rights of the American people, the media maintained the faulty system and the war on terror frame focusing on the belief that the police were handcuffed by the rules. The early days of the war on terror showed more support than opposition for the PATRIOT Act. However, as the nation was faced with the 2013 whistle-blowing activities of Edward Snowden, questions started to once again emerge about the abuses of the government. In this way, the faulty system became a corrupt system. Though the media are still inclined to portray the war on terror frame as a law enforcement responsibility that must be fought with drastic means, the debates continue.

Weblink 3.6

For a detailed discussion of terrorism and counterterrorism, visit the FBI: https://archives.fbi.gov/archives/news/testimony/the-terrorist-threat-confronting-the-united-states.

CONCLUSION

Sasson's framing typology was developed more than twenty years prior to the publication of this book. Sasson, and other media researchers, acknowledged that frames often overlap. Additionally, other media frames have been identified though not discussed here. However, all agree that media frames provide organization, meaning, and solutions. With changing cultural ideologies, images are bound to change in some form. Yet, the faulty system frame is one that has endured the test of time. As you can see from the various news stories we have shared throughout this chapter, frames do tend to overlap. It is not uncommon to find the faulty system frame as well as the social breakdown frame. However, when it comes to crime the media tend to narrate criminal justice limitations aligned with emphasis on individual or cultural deficiencies. This framing suggests that the required criminal justice policy is to "get tough on crime."

Considering solutions embedded in each of the frames, the blocked opportunities frame requires the government to create jobs and eliminate poverty. The social breakdown frame requires that communities rebuild traditional communities that are believed to control crime. The racist system frame requires that the oppressed band together and demand justice and equality. And the violent media frame requires that greater regulations be implemented to reduce violent media. However, these policies become muddied when we see overlapping frames within a given media image. When the faulty system and the war on terror frames are the overriding frames, we maintain a "get tough on crime" society.

Chapter 4

Crime in the Movies

SOCIAL CONSTRUCTION OF CRIME IN THE MOVIES

Media researchers have examined the making of news and images for decades. However, criminology did not begin to seriously analyze crime in the media until about the 1990s. Prominent media researchers in criminology include Theodore Sasson, Ray Surette, and the late Nicole Rafter. It is only in recent years that criminologists began to accept this field of research as useful to the discipline. Most notably, the rise of social media and its influence on the news and on public perception and activities has driven this focus. Unfortunately, criminology still has yet to acknowledge that crime viewed on television crime dramas and in the movies can have a large impact. The movie industry is a $38 billion box office industry and is predicted to increase to $49 billion by 2020.[1] The United States leads the film industry worldwide. Furthermore, some predict that revenue from online movie streaming may surpass box office sales since companies like Netflix, Amazon, and Hulu allow people to view movies for a lot less money.

The aforementioned facts have significance. The images that people are exposed to impact their perceptions and perceptions impact criminal justice policy. As discussed in Chapter 2, cultivation theory shows that the more people are exposed to the media, the more likely they are to internalize the messages and themes put forth.[2] When examining images of crime, James Hamilton found that people are more likely to fear for their safety and to be pessimistic about society. Furthermore, people who consume large amounts of violent media in entertainment crime programming and news are more likely to develop the "mean world" syndrome. That is, that society is not a good place and people are no good.

So we must ask ourselves, what are people being exposed to in crime movies? We examine the social constructs of crime in the movies. As described in Chapter 1, social construction theory argues that society, and its various institutions, provides simplified categorizations of people, interactions, and events in order to allow for understanding in a complex society. Most people do not have direct experience with crime and justice so they rely on social constructs to guide their understanding. Grossberg, Wartella, and Whitney show that the media are actively involved in making, or at least, guiding, and reinforcing our social images.[3] In this chapter, we examine images of crime, criminals, and justice officials within the ten highest grossing crime movies in the 2000s. We revisit the activities of framing and narrating crime that were discussed in Chapter 3.

Most of the research that examines framing of crime in the media focuses on news media. Framing, as defined in Chapter 3, is the prepackaging of social constructs that includes facts as well as interpretations of people and events, in this case involving crime, which can be linked to policies of crime control.[4] Media framing organizes crime and justice. It categorizes and labels crime and justice, allowing consumers to quickly learn in the same way as is done in the process of socially constructing reality. Researchers have found that these frames are a reflection of what is believed within the larger society.[5]

We can add movie media as part of the social construction process. As discussed in Chapter 3, media researchers have identified episodic frames and thematic frames. Episodic frames focus on an immediate event and are more likely to be seen in news media. Thematic frames, on the other hand, link current stories with previous stories providing a bigger picture or pattern of crime and justice.[6] Movies are more likely to rely on thematic frames since they can tell a story over a period of two or more hours and can take the audience through a character's lifetime.

In addition to crime frames, we obtain more detail with narratives. As described in Chapter 3, narratives outline the recurring crime-and-justice situations that regularly appear in the media.[7] Narratives provide the details of the story within the frame. They describe the characteristics of the criminals, victims, witnesses, and justice officials involved and how they interact within a given crime setting. Movies have a distinct advantage of providing narratives through the spoken and unspoken words of the actors as well as through visual representations. The problem with frames and narratives is that they do not expose us to competing frames and narratives. This results in a construction of the typical offender, the typical victim, and the typical justice official. In a racist and sexist society, both past and present, this results in reinforcing the image of the symbolic assailant and the innocent victim. The benefits of framing crime and justice in the movies are that they can take the time to reveal a complex and unfolding situation. This results in overlapping frames and can have the benefit of showing the audience different explanations of crime. So what are the frames and their accompanying narratives found in crime movies?

FRAMING THE CAUSES OF CRIME IN THE MOVIES

As detailed in Chapter 3, Sasson describes five widely accepted cultural frames on street crime that are widely accepted today. He named them (1) the faulty system, (2) blocked opportunities, (3) social breakdown, (4) the racist system, and (5) violent media. We also added the war on terror frame to the discussion. Using these frames, the movies tell us in much more detail than do the news media who is responsible for crime, why they commit these crimes, and which crime control policies are most effective. In this chapter we reintroduce these frames and apply them to crime movies. We must keep in mind that these frames were identified in the mid-1990s. Since then we have been in a war on terror and have increased our concern over immigrant crime.

The Faulty System

In the faulty system frame, crime is the result of an incompetent criminal justice system, a system unable to apprehend and punish rational, free-willed criminals. Movies of the 1970s and 1980s commonly used this theme as we were inundated with movie franchises such as *Death Wish*, *Die Hard*, *Dirty Harry*, and *Lethal Weapon*. This was an era on the tail end of civil unrest, a distrust of the government, and an increase in crime. Within this frame, dedicated detectives such as John McClane, Harry Callahan, Martin Riggs, and Roger Murtaugh try hard to catch the criminals but have their hands tied by rules that allow violent predators to go free.

This frame also shows that victims, such as *Death Wish*'s Paul Kersey, cannot be safe or cannot receive justice in a crime-ridden society because the police are incapable or incompetent. According to this movie frame, the only response is for a police officer to go rogue, for the police to look for more competent help outside of the department, or for victims to engage in vigilante justice. When we factor in Sasson's smaller subthemes, described in Chapter 3, we find that crime movies are much more likely to focus on the criminal and the process of crime investigation and apprehension. The handcuffed police describe the limits the courts have placed on the police which ties them down with offender due process rights. A common belief is that criminals do not deserve these rights because these rights deny justice to victims. To Sasson's subthemes, we can also add criminal justice "incompetence" and "corruption."

War on Terror

The war on terror frame has been used in the movies for decades. James Bond has been fighting terrorists from all over the world since the 1960s. Sean Connery and Nicholas cage fought domestic terrorists in *The Rock*. Harrison Ford fought Kazakhstanian terrorists in *Air Force One*. Many movies have also been produced portraying the war on terror since 9/11. These include very popular movies such as *American Snipper*, *Flight 93*, *Lone Survivor*, and *Zero Dark Thirty*. Since 9/11, this frame has strongly focused on Muslim terrorists. However, other war on terror movies have also hit the box office: *Jack Ryan: Shadow Recruit*, *Olympus Has Fallen*, *London Has Fallen*, *Sum of All Fears*, and *White House Down*. It is important to note that these latter movies do not focus on Islamic extremist terrorism but hold to the war on terror frame. In other words, the United States faces terror attacks from all fronts.

Blocked Opportunities

As discussed in Chapter 3, Sasson's blocked opportunities frame portrays crime as resulting from poverty and inequality. In this frame, criminals are innovators trying to gain wealth or retreat from poverty and oppression. Additionally, this frame can portray criminals as people with poor coping mechanisms responding to various life strains. In the movie, *Falling Down*, William "D-FENS" Foster (played by Michael Douglas) goes on a killing spree after losing his wife and his job. Movies abound with stories of blocked opportunities. The blocked opportunities frame can be found in movies such as *Ocean's Eleven*, *Heist*, *The Town*, and various organized crime movies such as *Gangs of New York*, *The Godfather*, *Godfellas*, and *The Departed*.

Social Breakdown

The social breakdown is another common frame used in crime movies, typically when focusing on urban crime. Sasson found that the social breakdown frame sees crime as resulting from broken families and communities. Crime movies provide both the conservative and the liberal ideologies within this frame. However, they tend to place greater focus on the conservative ideology with all of the attention given to the social relationships of the characters. In the acclaimed movie *Gran Torino*, Clint Eastwood's character is a bigot who holds to this conservative ideology accusing Asians (he does not acknowledge that there are Asian Americans) of being violent criminals. While Eastwood's character comes to understand that the proliferation of Asian gangs is much more complicated than he previously believed, the movie does not place enough emphasis on other explanations of social breakdown. It also loses the liberal ideology as it focuses on the extreme violence of the gang members. Some movies, however, maintain a stronger focus on the liberal ideology within the social breakdown frame by addressing blocked opportunities more fully. *Set It Off* depicts crime as the result of broken neighborhoods, poverty, and sexual and racial oppressions. Regardless, most agree that social breakdown can be rooted in the family as well as the neighborhood. Other movies using the social breakdown frame include *Menace II Society*, *Straight Outta Compton*, *Monster*, and *Get the Gringo*.

Racist System

The racist system frame can be found in many crime movies but typically not as the primary media frame. Movies often tell us that there would likely be a more equal racial representation in arrests, convictions, and sentences if not for the racism prevalent within the system. The racist system frame can be found in such current movies as *The Birth of a Nation* (2016), *Free State of Jones*, *Straight Outta Compton*, *Selma*, and *Crash*. While most of these movies are not listed in the crime genre, they address crime, and the crime can be explained in many cases by the racist system frame. We also often see the racist frame overlapped with social breakdown, such as in *Set It Off* and *Straight Outta Compton*, or with blocked opportunities, such as in *Get the Gringo*.

Violent Media

The violent media frame describes crimes as resulting from exposure to violence within all forms of media. According to this frame, people will follow media messages or become angry with what they see or hear in the media. When *Mississippi Burning* was released, a group of African American teenagers attacked a white teen out of anger stemmed from the movie. In this case (*Wisconsin v. Mitchell*), Todd Michell was given a four-year sentence, given that the crime constituted a hate crime and was defined by the U.S. Supreme Court to be worse than other crimes.[8] In *Nerve*, an online truth or dare game sparks violence that is accepted by a desensitized youth population. *Straight Outta Compton* shows the effects of gangsta rap in the mid-1980s and into the 1990s. However, it is more common today to find this theme within serial killer movies such as *CopyCat* and *Natural Born Killers*.

FRAMING AND NARRATING CRIME AND CRIMINALS IN THE MOVIES

Research that examines media framing has examined what crime occurs and why. The previous section examined framing *why* crime occurs. In this section, we examine framing *what* crime occurs. Because the field is relatively new to criminology, we do not find an agreed upon typology of crime frames. However, with a quick search of the research, as well as of movies, one can quickly see that crime frames focus predominantly on violent crimes. Common crime frames include terrorism, drug trafficking and, more recently, human trafficking, gang violence, organized crime, serial killing, and revenge killings. Within crime frames we can find the narratives of who commits these crimes and how their motives play out. Research on news media shows that when a violent crime occurs and the suspect is Muslim, there is an automatic assumption of terrorism.[9] Within the terror frame, we often find the faulty system frame in which the system failed to identify or monitor the offender. We also find a narrative of an extremist male Muslim who is willing to die for the cause. When we see nonviolent crimes in the media, they often involve heists resulting in millions of dollars stolen.

Nicole Rafter and Robert Ray describe the crime movie hero.[10] Throughout film-making history, crime heroes have been popular. Good-guy heroes (official heroes) tend to be law-abiding citizens and save the day. Robert Ray claimed that "the official hero, normally portrayed as a teacher, lawyer, politician, farmer, or family man, represented the American belief in collective action, and the objective legal process that superseded private notions of right and wrong."[11] Bad-guy heroes (outlaw heroes), however, tend to be more popular in the movie industry. Bad-guy heroes are tough and sometimes cruel. They break the law and defy authority. They do the things that law-abiding citizens sometimes fantasize doing. According to Robert Ray, the outlaw hero, typically an adventurer, gunfighter, or loner, represents American values of self-determination and freedom from entanglements.[12] Ray argues that we are comfortable liking the bad-guy hero because in the end they always die returning us to our moral comfort.

Rafter describes eight categories of crime heroes: sleuths, victim heroes, criminal masterminds, mistreated heroes, outsider heroes, avengers, criminal heroes, and superheroes. These heroes are often linked to specific crime movie subgenres: mysteries/detective stories, thrillers, capers and heists, justice violated/justice restored, disguised Westerns, revenge/vigilante, chronicles of criminal careers, and action. Sleuths, generally found in mysteries and detective movies, are very intelligent, persistent, and imaginative. Though these heroes may be police detectives, they are typically amateurish (*Veronica Mars*) or eccentric (*Sherlock Holmes*), and they are typically able to solve that which the police cannot. Victim heroes are typically found in thrillers and are ordinary people who suddenly find themselves in a dire situation. These victims often find themselves in a kill or be killed situation (i.e., Detective Costigan in *The Departed*). Criminal masterminds, typically found in caper and heist movies, are somewhat of a quandary. These heroes are typically the criminals we love and cheer on. They are masterminds of their trade and oftentimes rob the rich or the worse criminal. Criminal masterminds earn their right to center stage by their regal persona or the nobleness of their cause (*Tower Heist* and *Heist*). Mistreated heroes are often found in justice violated/justice restored movies and may be innocent victims (victim heroes) or tainted individuals. As Rafter describes, they may be "compromised characters, guilty of something but undeserving of the suffering they currently endure."[13] Throughout the movie they work very hard to clear their name. Jason Bourne of the *Bourne* movies franchise is a prime example of this hero.

Outsider heroes are typically found in disguised Westerns. Disguised Westerns are very similar to traditional Westerns but do not take place in the old West. In these movies, an outsider is brought in or stumbles into a situation of extreme exploitation or crime. The outsider hero is self-sacrificing and often comes in guns blazing in order to fight for the helpless victim. *The Equalizer* is a prime example of a modern-day outsider hero in a disguised Western. Avengers can be found in revenge/vigilante movies. These heroes pursue the bad guys for personal reasons. They are patient, highly capable, and have years of experience. *Man on Fire, Kill Bill, Payback*, and *The Brave One* were hit revenge/vigilante movies in which the avengers were unstoppable in planning and obtaining revenge against their aggressors or surrogate criminals.

Criminal heroes can be found in chronical career criminal movies as well as in caper/heist movies. In earlier movies, they were typically gangsters. In noirs, they were shady detectives and other such criminal characters such as lovers and corrupt cops. Today, the most common criminal heroes can be found in caper/heist movies, and they tend not to be violent or overly violent. Unlike Ray's earlier claims that the bad-guy hero tends to be killed off, today's heroes tend to survive and even escape severe punishment. Some popular criminal heroes of today can be found in movies like *Takers, Leon: The Professional, Public Enemies, Inception*, and *Pulp Fiction*.

Action movie heroes are known as superheroes and tend to be the most popular crime movie heroes today. The box office has seen much more success with this crime subgenre. Action heroes are portrayed as invincible. They can be good-guy heroes or bad-good guy heroes. The good-guy hero tends to be the superhero cop, whereas the bad-guy hero tends to be the criminal hero. Superheroes can survive high falls and car crashes, escape bullets and explosions, and take on a crowd of professional killers. Examples of movies with good-guy superheroes include *Die Hard, Lethal Weapon, True Lies*, and *Mission Impossible*. Examples of movies with bad-guy superheroes include *The Fast and the Furious, The Bourne Identity*, and *The Transporter*.

TOP GROSSING U.S. CRIME MOVIES

To further explore crime frames and narratives, we examined the ten highest-grossing U.S. crime films of the current century. Movies are identified as crime movies because their plot revolves around a crime or a series of crimes. The crime movie genre can be divided into several subgenres. Popular crime movie genres found in the literature can be broken down into whodunnit/ detective movies, hardboiled detective movies, gangster movies, and court-room/legal thriller movies. Crime movies can overlap the action movie sub-genre and can include epic movies, spy movies, disaster movies, superhero movies, thrillers, martial arts movies, and video game/comic book movies. Here we do not examine superhero, martial arts, and video game/comic book movies. Where movies had sequels, we viewed the highest-grossing movie. For example, in the *Fast and Furious* franchise, we viewed *Furious 7* (2015). We also excluded comedies as they tend to minimize the criminal focus and overly exaggerate deficiencies within or strengths of the criminal justice system. We also excluded the serial killer movie as this movie category tends to need a more in-depth examination. In our examination, we allowed for the overlap of epic, spy, and thriller movies. Table 4.1 presents how much each of the selected movies grossed. Subgenres tend to be flexible. The research shows that the gangster/organized crime subgenre that was popular in the 1930s and then again in the 1970s is the most popular crime subgenre today. Six of the ten highest-grossing movies are action movies. Only one is a detective movie, one a true crime, and one a historical drama.

FRAMING THE CAUSES OF CRIME IN THE MOVIES

As we examine the movie frames of why the crimes occur, we see that there is an overlap of mostly the faulty system and blocked opportunities frames. *American Hustle*, *Bad Boys II*, *Furious 7*, *Ocean's Eleven*, *Sherlock Holmes*, *Taken 2*, and *The Departed*, all follow these two frames. Additionally, while *Furious 7* and *Sherlock Holmes* also include a terrorism frame, the movies do not place much emphasis on the crimes as terrorism. Table 4.2 lists the primary and secondary frames of these movies. Most of these movies use blocked opportunities as the primary frame. *The Departed* utilizes the faulty system frame as the primary frame and the blocked opportunities as the secondary frame. Throughout this movie, law enforcement works endlessly to capture the criminals, always to be evaded. Similarly, *Bad Boys II* uses the faulty system frame as the primary frame and blocked opportunities as the secondary frame. In the remaining movies, the stories center on the criminals' activities and their motives. Apprehension by the police is incidental. While

Table 4.1. Top Ten U.S. Grossing Crime Films, 2000–2015

Movie*	IMDB Subgenre	Criminology Subgenre	Gross in Millions (in dollars)
2. *Furious 7* (2015)	Action/crime/thriller	Gangster/organized crime Terrorism	533
8. *Sherlock Holmes* (2009)	Action/adventure/ crime	Hardboiled detective Terrorism	209
12. *Mr. & Mrs. Smith* (2005)	Action/comedy/crime	Gangster/organized crime	186
14. *Ocean's Eleven* (2001)	Crime/thriller	Heist	183
16. *Gone Girl* (2014)	Crime/drama/mystery	Noir	168
18. *Catch Me If You Can* (2014)	Biography/crime/ drama	Caper	164
26. *American Hustle* (2013)	Crime/drama/ historical	Caper Gangster/organized crime	150
32. *Taken 2* (2012)	Action/crime/thriller	Gangster/organized crime	140
35. *Bad Boys II* (2003)	Action/comedy/crime	Cop Gangster/organized crime	138
41. *The Departed* (2006)	Crime/drama/thriller	Cop Gangster/organized crime	132

Note: *The numbering in this column indicates where the movie is listed in the Top-US-Grossing Feature Films.

the violent media and racist system frames can be found in crime movies today, they did not make the top ten. We warn you now that spoiler alerts can be found within this chapter! For you movie lovers, read at your own peril!

Blocked Opportunities/Faulty System

As described by Sasson, blocked opportunities are rooted in strain theory. Accordingly, people who cannot gain wealth through legitimate means may attempt to obtain wealth through crime. This is a common theme within crime movies. We found that the blocked opportunities frame is often coupled with the faulty system frame in today's movies. While Sasson found that support for blocked opportunities was often accompanied by rejection of the faulty system and vice versa, he was examining op-ed news pieces and public responses to them.[14] As Nicole Rafter and Michelle Brown point out in their book *Criminology Goes to the Movies*, film has the ability to provide complex

Table 4.2. Primary and Secondary Frames: Why Crime Occurs

Movie	Primary Frame	Secondary Frame	Plot
American Hustle	Blocked opportunities	Faulty system	Con artist couple, desperate to survive and evade FBI
Bad Boys II	Faulty system	Blocked opportunities	International organized criminals who are extremely violent and allude police
Catch Me If You Can	Faulty system	Social breakdown	Highly intelligent self-taught boy/man who evades law enforcement
Gone Girl	Social breakdown	Faulty system	Femme fatale, mentally unstable scorned woman who will stop at nothing to control her cheating husband
Furious 7	Blocked opportunities	Faulty system/ war on terror	Former daredevil, self-taught street criminals who are more competent than police
Mr. & Mrs. Smith	Blocked opportunities	Social breakdown	Highly sophisticated contract killers who can shoot past any obstacle
Ocean's Eleven	Blocked opportunities	Faulty system	Highly sophisticated thieves who can bypass any private and public security
Sherlock Holmes	Blocked opportunities	Faulty system	Mastermind criminal who can only be apprehended by private detectives
Taken 2	Blocked opportunities	Faulty system	Human traffickers willing to do anything for revenge who can only be stopped by a former CIA
The Departed	Faulty system	Blocked opportunities	Irish mob boss who infiltrates the police

explanations of crime that one theory is incapable of doing.[15] In one pattern of frame integration, thieves are chased down by the police but are too clever to be caught.

In *American Hustle*, Sydney Prosser (played by Amy Adams) desperately wants to be someone. She teams up with Irving Rosenfeld (played by Christian Bale) posing as British royalty in order to con desperate people out of money. Sydney and Irving grew up without much money and did not mind conning people to gain their wealth. In narration, Irving describes his childhood reaction to seeing how his father was victimized in the glass business:

> I would rather be on the taking side than the getting taken side any day of the week after I saw how my father got taken.

Sydney meets Irving, who has a wife and child, at a party where they find a common interest in Duke Wellington. In narration, Sydney describes:

> I was broke, fearless, with nothing to lose. And my dream, more than anything, was to become anyone else other than who I was.

Together Sydney and Irving proceed to con people in loan and art scams. They work successfully until they meet FBI agent Richie DiMaso (played by Bradley Cooper). Agent DiMaso pressures them into helping the FBI take down four corrupt officials or white collar criminals in exchange for immunity. Through this partnership, Sydney and Irving seem to be trapped working out ways to "survive." Here their strain is reflected in Robert Agnew's general strain theory in which they experience the introduction of a negative event. Sydney devises a plan to trap Agent DiMaso in a sensual web and throughout the movie the pair appear to be in a relationship. Yet, we see that the FBI is not reaping much benefit. Sydney and Irving are pulled in deeper, being forced to work with the Italian mafia, yet another negative event introduced into their lives. In the end, the couple con the FBI out of $2 million, win their freedom, and escape the clutches of the mafia. Their con on the FBI allows them to achieve those once blocked goals. Additionally, the faulty system that is the FBI is unable to keep up with the con artists who first con for money and excitement and then con to survive. As Irving states, "The art of survival is a story that never ends."

The con artists in *American Hustle* live for the excitement of the con. Similarly, the thieves of *Ocean's Eleven* relish planning and pulling off the biggest heist in Las Vegas's history. Here we see evidence of rational choice theory that is most closely linked to the faulty system frame. However, achieving the goals of excitement and $150 million in the heist are the most important aspects of the movie. Most of the thieves are not wealthy people. While the economic backgrounds are not portrayed within the movie, one gets the idea that all except Reuben, a former casino owner, would be poor or working class if not for their crimes. They plan the heist with calm expertise that is unquestionably superior to anything or anyone put in place to stop them. Danny Ocean (played by George Clooney) is the leader of the group with the close assistance of Rusty Ryan (played by Brad Pitt). They are classy and calm and live for the heist. But they are not powerful men. They are gambling men. Rusty even teaches people to gamble. Danny Ocean is also a gambling man. He narrates:

> The house always wins. . . . Unless that perfect hand comes along, you bet big and you take the house.

In the opening scene, when Danny Ocean is asked by the parole board why he committed his crime, he responds,

My wife left me, I was upset. I was in a self-destructive pattern.

Although we quickly learn that Danny Ocean plans the casino heist because the owner is dating his ex-wife, explained by general strain theory, we see that the excitement of the heist and the money are very much coveted. In either case, both are blocked opportunities for Danny Ocean.

Although there are no elaborate scenes stressing law enforcement activities, we are presented with two scenes that show the incompetence of law enforcement when faced with the criminal expertise of Danny Ocean's crew. In one scene, Rusty impersonates an ATF agent and intimidates a police officer into leaving him alone with the bank robber, Basher (player by Don Cheadle), allowing him to escape arrest. In a second scene, the team's technical expert, Livingston (played by Eddie Jemison), impersonates an emergency operator, allowing the crew to impersonate a S.W.A.T. team. However, throughout the heist we see that even the tightest security cannot stop Ocean's crew of thieves. All of this points to a faulty system.

Other movies that use the blocked opportunities/faulty system frames tend to be more violent. In *Bad Boys II*, international drug dealers are fighting for territory in Miami, Florida. Johnny Tapia (played by Jordi Molla) is a Cuban drug lord who is extremely violent and psychologically unstable. He will kill anyone who jeopardizes his operation, including his own men. Alexei (played by Peter Stormare) is a Russian drug lord who is in competition with the Cuban organized crime group. They both commit their crimes for the massive wealth obtained and murder senselessly in the course of doing so. The movie, however, is a cop movie and centers on Detectives Mike Lowrey (played by Will Smith) and Marcus Burnett (played by Martin Lawrence). While Mike and Marcus eventually bring down Tapia's criminal empire, they make many mistakes along the way. The faulty system is reflected in faulty intelligence, broken radios, reckless car chases, and accidentally ingesting drugs. After Tapia kidnaps Marcus Burnett's sister, who is a DEA agent, and flies to Cuba, the Miami Police Department is told that they cannot pursue Tapia due to jurisdictional boundaries. At this point, Detectives Lowrey and Burnett, along with several other detectives and a CIA agent, go rogue and enter Cuban jurisdiction. When Detective Mike Lowrey sees that his partner plans to go to Cuba to rescue his sister, he reminds Detective Burnett of their childhood motto: "We ride together, we die together, Bad Boys for life." The Bad Boys are now officially criminals. However, they are still portrayed as superhero cops as they shoot their way through Johnny Tapia's Cuban estate and a corrupt Cuban army.

Furious 7 follows the blocked opportunities/faulty system frames. The complexity of *Furious 7* is that Dominic Toretto (played by Vin Diesel) and his crew are introduced as a criminal street racing crew in the first movie. At that time, they are investigated by Los Angeles police officer Brian O'Conner (played by Paul Walker) who goes native and becomes corrupt. Sequels to the first movie show the crew committing various crimes. And running from authorities in various parts of the world. In *Furious 7*, the crew is recruited by a clandestine government agent to retrieve dangerous technology from African terrorist Mose Jakande (played by Djimon Hounsou). In the movie, terrorist Jakande and Special Forces Deckard Shaw (played by Jason Strathem) are the criminals. In the *Furious* franchise, Toretto's group is criminal, yet in *Furious 7*, they are the only ones who can stop terrorist Jakande. Jakande wants to control intelligence stealing technology called God's Eye, and the government is incapable of getting the job done (faulty system). Jakande's blocked opportunity is the power he desires. Shaw's blocked opportunity is getting revenge against the crew who severely injured his criminal brother in the previous movie. In turn, Toretto's crew faces the strain that Shaw is trying to kill them. If they can stop Jakande and obtain the God's Eye, they can locate Shaw and stop him. As described, Jakande is a terrorist, or a cyberterrorist. However, the movie only alludes to the war on terror frame.

Similarly, Sherlock Holmes is the only one who can figure out the puzzles of Lord Blackwood (played by Mark Strong) and Professor Moriarty. In the movie *Sherlock Holmes*, Holmes (played by Robert Downing, Jr.) and his friend and partner Dr. Watson (played by Jude Law) first must discover who is killing women in a sacrificial manner which seems to be rooted in dark magic. Scotland Yard is unable to solve the crimes (faulty system) and must rely on the private investigators. Holmes and Watson identify and capture the serial killer, Lord Blackwood. Lord Blackwood is hung for his crimes but comes back to life to continue his killing spree. When police officers are too afraid to enter Blackwood's tomb, Inspector Lestrade points out their incompetence when he scolds his men:

> If you all don't stop behaving like a bunch of quivering milk maids, you're on double time.

Holmes, with the help of Watson, once again is the only one who can solve the mystery. Holmes and Watson learn that Blackwood and the Temple of the Four Orders are trying to destroy British Parliament and take over the country. Their motive is power (blocked opportunity). Blackwood introduces his plans to take over England, the American Colonies, and the world,

My powers and my assets were given to me for one purpose, a simple purpose, to create a new future. A future ruled by us.

In an act of terrorism, Blackwood and his brethren plan to murder the members of Parliament. Blackwood informs Parliament that those who follow him and his order will live while all others will die,

Listen to the fear. I will use that as a weapon to control them and then the world.

In the course of their investigation, Holmes and Watson learn that many government officials are corrupt (faulty system). Once again, Holmes and Watson apprehend Blackwood but only with some assistance from Scotland Yard. In framing of the crimes, while we know by the end that terrorism is a factor, it is not explicitly addressed in the movie as such so we did not assign that frame.

Taken 2 centers on revenge of an Albanian organized crime group that specializes in human trafficking. In the first movie, the daughter of Liam Neeson's character Bryan Mills is kidnapped by an Albanian criminal syndicate. Mills, being a highly trained retired CIA agent, pursues his daughter leaving dead bodies in his wake, including the son of Murad Krasniqi (played by Rade Serbedzija), the leader of the Albanian organized crime group. *Taken 2* opens with the funeral of the dead Albanian gangsters. During the funeral, Krasniqi shows the intense strain he is experiencing when he declares:

He slaughtered our men, our brothers, our sons. The dead cry out to us for justice. On their souls, I swear to you, the man who took our loved ones from us, the man who has brought us such pain and sorrow; we will find him. We will bring him here. We will not rest until his blood flows into this very ground. We will have our revenge.

Krasniqi proceeds to kidnap Mills and his wife Lenore (played by Famke Janssen) during a trip to Istanbul. His men kill indiscriminately trying to also kidnap Mills's daughter Kim (played by Maggie Grace). Kim helps Mills escape. In a brief scene, it is made apparent that a high official within the Istanbul Police Department is working for Krasniqi (faulty system). This brief scene easily explains why Mills fails to contact the police and handles the rescue of his wife by himself. Though the audience is left rooting for Mills's success, it should be noted that his behaviors are also criminal and can be explained by the blocked opportunities and the faulty system frames.

The Departed opens with Irish mob boss Frank Costello (played by Jack Nicholson) describing how Boston used to be. He describes the racial tension and the poverty of Boston's past (blocked opportunities). He claims:

The Church wants you in your place: kneel, stand, kneel, stand. Man makes his own way. Twenty years after the Irish couldn't get a fuckin' job, we had the Presidency. No one gives it to you. You have to take it.

Detective Sullivan (played by Matt Damon) is shown growing up in poverty and in awe of Frank Castello. Initially, it appears that we may have to use the social breakdown frame. However, the movie quickly places the focus on blocked opportunities, "No one gives it to you. You have to take it." The movie centers on Costello trying to maintain his power and wealth through crime and by infiltrating the Boston Police Department. In adulthood, we see Detective Sullivan buying an expensive condominium with a view of the Massachusetts State House. Sullivan is on the take, on his way to law school, and has goals to make it to the state house. However, his goals are blocked by the police and undercover officer Costigan (played by Leonardo DiCaprio) in Costello's network. The movie goes around in circles as Costello's men try to identify the "rat" in the organization and the Boston police try to identify Costello's mole in the department. While there is a strong use of the blocked opportunities frame, the movie continuously returns to the faulty system frame with the corrupt police department and the FBI who allow the Irish mob to thrive.

Faulty System/Social Breakdown

Two of the top ten highest grossing movies use the faulty system frame with the social breakdown frame. As described earlier, crime is the result of the breakdown of traditional values, the family, and the community. When there is breakdown, the institutions within society are unable to control criminal behavior. In *Catch Me If You Can* (based on a true story), sixteen-year-old Frank Abagnale, Jr. (played by Leonardo DiCaprio) runs away from home upon learning about his parents' plan to divorce. Within a three-year period, Abagnale impersonates an airplane pilot, a lawyer, and a doctor all while scamming companies out of millions of dollars. The movie shows that Frank has learned his con games and money fraud from his father. He also learns about deceit after he learns that his mother is having an affair. When Frank's parents ask him to choose who he wants to live with, he can no longer deal with his family's breakdown and runs away. At one point, he tries to unite them with the money he has stolen but fails. All of this points to social breakdown.

Almost from the beginning Frank is pursued by FBI agent Carl Hanratty, Jr. (played by Tom Hanks). Agent Hanratty tirelessly pursues Frank, but his superiors do not place much importance on his crimes (faulty system). For three years, Agent Hanratty pursues Frank with a lack of support from his superiors. It was not until the French police caught Frank that Agent Hanratty was able to gain custody.

Gone Girl is a different type of crime movie. In this noir, as with many, you do not know who the criminal is for some time. However, as the story unfolds, we learn that Amy Dunne (played by Rosamund Pike) is not kidnapped by her husband Nick Dunne (played by Ben Affleck). In fact, Amy fakes her kidnapping, framing her husband as revenge for cheating on her and using her for her money. It is obvious that Amy suffers mental illness as she kills heartlessly. However, the movie does provide strong sociological evidence that her family of orientation was dysfunctional as her mother publicized every major achievement in her life for her *Amazing Amy* books. Amy, known as Amazing Amy, had her life on display and hated it. We also learn that the breakdown of her marriage was the trigger to her current crimes. However, Amy has falsely accused past boyfriends of rape and stalking and was able to convince the police of her victimizations. Unfortunately, Amy is never captured because the police keep their focus on Nick as the culprit (faulty system). They are not willing or able to see that this amazing woman could possibly fake her own kidnapping or murder another human being.

Blocked Opportunities/Social Breakdown

Mr. & Mrs. Smith is a very action-packed movie with lots of violence and some humor. In this movie, the audience is never given the idea that they should not like the Smiths. The Smiths are hired assassins whose work is portrayed as a normal nine-to-five job. It is not until they are assigned to the same contract that their true identities become known to each other and to their employers. They begin by trying to determine their real identities and then trying to kill or not be killed by the other. While their jobs are normalized, their violence toward each other is portrayed as a result of the breakdown of their family of procreation. We are only given a glimpse of their childhood when Jane tells John that her parents died when she was five and that she is an orphan. They are married for "five or six" years before their true identities are discovered. They soon learn that Jane Smith (played by Angelina Jolie) is not the career/homemaker she pretends to be, while John Smith (played by Brad Pitt) is not the working man he pretends to be. The Smiths realize that their family is a lie (social breakdown). In *Mr. & Mrs. Smith*, we cannot point to a faulty system because the police are never involved; they are not even mentioned.

Instead, we can see the blocked opportunity frame when their employers have learned of their true identities and want them killed. Their employers learn that Jane and John are each working for the competition. This fact serves as blockage to the reputation and financial success of each corporation. Further, the need to survive is blocked by the hired killers their employers send.

CRIME FRAMES AND NARRATIVES

Aside from *American Hustle, Catch Me If You Can*, and *Ocean's Eleven*, most box office crime hits tend to be very violent. Table 4.3 reveals crime

Table 4.3. Crime and Narratives Frames

Movie	Crime Frame	Narrative
American Hustle	Loan scam	• Con artist couple • The corrupt FBI agent
Bad Boys II	Drug dealing, murder	International organized criminals (Cuban and Russian)
Catch Me If You Can	Bank fraud, illegal impersonations	Teenage con artist
Gone Girl	Murder	Femme fatale
Furious 7	• Revenge killing • Cyberterrorism, murder	• Special forces rogue • African terrorist
Mr. & Mrs. Smith	Contract killing	Assassin couple/organized crime
Ocean's Eleven	Theft	Group of highly trained thieves
Sherlock Holmes	Domestic terrorism, murder	Mastermind criminal/corruption
Taken 2	Kidnapping, murder	Albanian human traffickers/corruption
The Departed	• Murder, drug dealing • Murder, corruption	• Corrupt police • Irish mob

frames and their accompanying narratives. We can see that seven of the ten top grossing movies use violent crime frames. Murder is the most common crime frame committed mostly by organized criminals but also includes highly competent criminals such as former Special Forces Deckard Shaw, as well as terrorist Mose Jakande in *Furious 7*, mentally unstable femme fatale Amy Dunne in *Gone Girl*, and mastermind terrorists Lord Blackwood and Professor James Moriarty in *Sherlock Holmes*. In all cases, the murderer is ruthless, highly capable, if not highly intelligent, and almost unstoppable.

Theft also seems to be popular as the fourth, sixth, and fourteenth highest grossing movies featured this frame. Thieves in these movies steal money amounting in the millions (*American Hustle, Catch Me If You Can,* and *Ocean's Eleven*). Furthermore, while murderers are portrayed as ruthlessly violent, thieves in these narratives tend to be likeable, nonviolent, and highly capable. They are highly intelligent, know all of the angles, and are able to avoid detection or serious punishment. The boy-next-door Frank Abagnale (*Catch Me If You Can*) was able to steal millions and elude the FBI for years as a teenager. Sydney Prosser (*American Hustle*) had a beauty, look of innocence (when she was not dressed promiscuously), and loyalty that reeled in her victims. And Danny Ocean and Rusty Ryan (*Ocean's Eleven*) each had a regal quality, intelligence, and confidence that made them likeable. Because these criminals do not physically harm others and often come from poverty, we do not see them as so bad. And while there have been many terrorism movies released since 9/11, only two of the ten highest-grossing crime movies involved terrorism. Yet, the narratives did not involve Islamic terrorists as is more common in television crime dramas and the war on terror was not the main focus.

Corruption was a common narrative. *American Hustle, Sherlock Holmes, Taken 2*, and *The Departed* had clear cases of police/government corruption. FBI agent Richie DiMaso, in *American Hustle*, was so driven in his crime fighting goal and so attracted to con artist Sydney Prosser that he fell into his own trap using drugs and finding backdoors in order to capture the "bad guys." While Inspector Lestrade in *Sherlock Holmes* initially appears to be corrupt, we learn that he is good, whereas Scotland Yard executioner was corrupt and Parliament was riddled with corruption. *Taken 2* reveals a high-level Istanbul police official working for the Albanian crime syndicate. In *The Departed*, corruption is so rampant that the audience is made to wonder throughout the movie who is not corrupt. Additionally, while *Bad Boys II* did not portray the lead detectives as corrupt, many of their activities were in fact illegal and, therefore, corrupt.

Criminal couples have not lost their attraction as a narrative in crime movies. Like *Bonnie and Clyde*, criminal couples are often still portrayed as likeable. *Mr. & Mrs. Smith* (third highest-grossing crime movie) presents a male–female contract killer couple. The couple spends the entire movie trying to kill each other and then running from their employers. Although they kill for a living, the audience finds themselves drawn in to the couple's cause and roots for their survival. In *American Hustle* (seventh highest-grossing crime movie), the con artist couple is consistently portrayed as trying to survive the corrupting hand of the FBI. Once again, the audience is left rooting for their ultimate con to work. And while *Furious 7* does not center on a criminal couple, they do give a lot of screen time to Toretto and Letty, a likeable couple within the criminal crew.

CRIME HEROES

Within the movies we viewed, the superhero was the most common narrative of crime heroes (see table 4.4). Five movies portrayed this type of character, and three of the five movies involved the good-guy hero. Holmes and Watson are the heroes in S*herlock Holmes*. These sleuths are shown as superheroes. Each is able to fight off several men at once, even an overly large one. They can survive a jump from buildings several stories high as well as explosions. Irene Adler is also portrayed as a hero. She is a bad-guy criminal hero. Although she works for Professor Moriarty and steals for him, in the end she aids Holmes and Watson in their efforts to stop the terrorist plot fashioned by Lord Blackwood. She too can survive explosions and outrun bullets. However, contrasting Robert Ray, this bad-guy hero survives and even escapes.

Table 4.4. Narratives of Crime Heroes

Plot Type	Crime Heroes	Movies
Mystery and detective (1)	Sleuths	*Sherlock Holmes*
Thrillers (1)	Victim heroes	*Gone Girl*
Capers/heists (3)	Criminal masterminds	*American Hustle, Catch Me If you Can,* and *Ocean's Eleven*
Justice violated/justice returned (2)	Mistreated heroes	*Gone Girl* and *The Departed*
Disguised Westerns (1)	Outsider heroes	*Furious 7*
Revenge and vigilante (3)	Avengers	*Bad Boys II, Sherlock Holmes,* and *Taken 2*
Chronicles of criminal careers (3)	Criminal heroes	*American Hustle, Catch Me If you Can,* and *Ocean's Eleven*
Action crime (5)	Superheroes	*Bad Boys II, Furious 7, Mr. & Mrs. Smith, Sherlock Holmes,* and *Taken 2*

In fact, most bad-guy heroes today are so likeable that they escape any kind of punishment.

In *Bad Boys II* (superheroes and avengers) we have two good-guy heroes who are detectives. As superheroes they are able to endure extreme violence and cleverly avoid sprays of bullets. In *Taken 2* (superhero and avenger) retired CIA agent Brian Mills is highly capable with technology, explosions, and hand-to-hand combat. Until the end fight, he typically appears to be unfazed when fighting killers. These good-guy heroes can be categorized as avengers since they often find themselves in trouble with the law for their extreme and illegal tactics. All but the detectives in *Bad Boys II* find themselves either arrested at one point or chased by the police.

The rest of the heroes are bad-guy heroes. *Gone Girl* (victim and mistreated hero) toes the line between hero and no hero. In this movie, Nick Dunne is suspicious and is initially unlikeable as he cheats and uses his wife for her money. However, as we learn the true nature of the Amy Dunne's disappearance, Nick becomes the victim who works tirelessly to bring Amy to justice. Although he is able to clear his name of murder, Nick loses in the end as his wife's cleverness once again traps him. Caper/heist movies often have bad-guy heroes. In *American Hustle* (criminal masterminds and criminal heroes), Sydney Prosser and Irving Rosenfeld, two very ambitious, smart, and successful con artists, scheme to escape the clutches of an increasingly corrupt and controlling FBI agent. They are able to get away with their crimes and live happily ever after. Similarly, Frank Abagnale, Jr. in *Catch Me If You Can* (criminal mastermind) superbly cons companies out of millions of dollars while only a teenager. He is nice to everyone he meets and even befriends the FBI agent chasing him. While he is eventually caught and incarcerated, he is released early in order to work for the FBI (criminal hero). In *Ocean's Eleven* (criminal masterminds), the audience is immediately drawn to a like-able Danny Ocean and Rusty Ryan. Ocean's crew plans the biggest casino heist against an owner who uses questionable business tactics. Although Danny Ocean is eventually arrested and incarcerated for parole violation, he and his crew get away with $150 million and Danny gets the woman.

CONCLUSION

The box office is very big business. Today's crime movies are not much different from the movies of yesterday. We find similar crime frames such as blocked opportunities and the faulty system. We still idolize criminals, and we still have more bad-guy heroes than good-guy heroes. Throughout history, the media have been critical of the criminal justice system, and today is not much different. However, since the day of *Dirty Harry* (1971), movies are more likely to portray police as superheroes than as bumbling idiots.

What does this mean in light of the social construction of crime and justice? We know that perception influences criminal justice policy. We know that media influences perception. We also know that the more exposure to violent media, the more likely are people to develop the mean-world syndrome. We tend to believe that society is riddled with violent crime and corrupt officials. Since the 1980s, we have seen passage of "get tough" crime control policies and mass incarceration.[16] Many ask the chicken-egg question. Which came first: the movie images of incredible violence and corruption or perceptions of incredible violence and corruption? Many media scholars point to the production of such movies in response to social changes.[17] As social constructionists, we argue that it is a cultural model of communication in which the media communicate that which already exists within society.[18]

Chapter 5

Crime Television

CRIME ON PRIMETIME

One must never forget to discuss television when looking at crime in the media. Crime framing and narration on television has taken several forms. In this chapter, we will discuss the television crime series. Television crime series are defined as any television program that has crime as its main focus and airs in regular intervals, usually weekly. In the past, crime dramas have always come to mind when thinking about crime on television. Just like in the movies, television crime shows fall into various genres. The most common genres include police procedurals, legal procedurals, courtroom dramas, prison dramas, and organized crime/career criminal dramas. Furthermore, similar to crime heroes in the movies, television crime shows tend to have heroes. The more common hero is the police officer or detective. Police procedurals, such as *Castle*,[1] follow the police through their investigations. These shows may place most of the focus on the police or they may dedicate a lot of screen time to the suspects and criminals narrating the motives and character of the criminal. Courtroom dramas dedicate a lot of screen time to the courtroom proceedings, such as *Perry Mason*, whereas legal procedurals give much more focus to the lawyers as the main investigators, for example, *Suit*. *Law & Order* and *Chicago Justice* are a mix of police procedural and courtroom drama, with the two halves working as a well-orchestrated team. However, the rest of the *Law & Order* franchise shows the prosecutors on occasion working with police.

Television also approaches crime and crime detection through the eyes of the criminal. Prison series are not that popular. However, shows such as *Prison Break* and *Orange Is the New Black* have brought a level of popularity to this subgenre and present the story through the eyes of the criminal. Series such as *Dexter*, *Breaking Bad*, and *White Collar* have become increasingly popular. As we discussed in the previous chapter, the audience often identifies with the struggles and defiance of the criminal. Crime series can also follow the *whodunnit* detective series. In this genre, you will find that an amateur sleuth is more capable of solving crimes than the police, such as in *Castle*, *Perception*, *Elementary*, and *Monk*.

It appears that among primetime television viewers, police procedurals and *whodunnit* series are the most popular. Nielson's ratings identify that, in the beginning of 2017, four of the top ten shows were crime series. *NCIS* was the most watched crime show, *NCIS: Los Angeles* was the third, *Bull* (starring former *NCIS* star Michael Weatherly) was fourth, and *NCIS: New Orleans* was eighth.[2] Nielson ratings also found that for the entire 2016, four of the ten regularly watched primetime TV programs were crime series involving police procedurals or legal procedurals: #2 *NCIS*, #5 *Bull*, #6 *NCIS: New Orleans*, and #10 *Blue Bloods*.[3]

Crime television is big business. In addition to watching the news to obtain information on crime, the public tends to rely on crime programs on television. Viewership runs into the millions on a weekly basis. The unfortunate fact is that while the audience knows that television crime programs are typically fiction, many tend to see them as representative of our society.[4] Researchers have continuously examined the question, does the media influence the viewer? This question has been examined by psychologists and media researchers for decades. Remember the Bobo doll experiment discussed in Chapter 4. Yet, while we have some evidence that television viewing has some effects on the viewers, we are still left to wonder how much influence crime television has and how direct this influence is on its audience.

CULTIVATING PERCEPTIONS OF CRIME THROUGH TELEVISION

In order to examine these questions, we must return once again to cultivation theory. Remember that cultivation theory claims that the more we are exposed to the media, the more likely we are to internalize their messages. Jockel and Fruh examine cultivation theory in order to understand how crime television exposure results in mean world beliefs. Jockel and Fruh tell us that there exists first-order cultivation and second-order cultivation.[5] First-order cultivation refers to the general beliefs about the world around us that are learned from frequent media exposure. This includes what we believe are the facts (i.e., social facts) about crime and justice. If television crime presents overwhelmingly violent crimes, then first-order cultivation results in a distorted perception of violent crime. Second-order cultivation, on the other hand, results in the attitudes and evaluations about social conditions that result from frequent media exposure. As such, an individual who is an advent viewer of *CSI* and *Dexter* is more likely to believe that there are a lot of very bad people in the world and only a few heroes, that is, the police. This belief is known as the mean-world syndrome.

Yet, cultivation is not so simple that frequent viewing of crime television is all that is required to influence perceptions of social facts and belief systems. The types of programs we gravitate to are also influenced by our personal ideologies or, as Jockel and Fruh indicate, by our moral foundation. People who are more politically conservative are more likely to be attracted to crime genres, though not all. This results in genre-specific cultivation; that is, our ideas of the world become narrower relying on limited messages of crime and justice. Media cultivation results in a re-enforcing spiral. So, conservatives are likely to be drawn to crime television and crime television reinforces conservativism.

Conservatives tend to have an unyielding moral foundation holding to law and order. At the same time, crime television tends to focus much more on law and order.[6] The law and order ideology views society as black and white, good and evil. When a person breaks the law, the law must act swiftly, certainly, and severely, otherwise, we risk chaos. While liberals and conservatives have always had a relatively balancing place in society, conservative ideologies have driven the practices of law and justice within the United States for many decades. Similarly, crime television has increasingly become law and order-oriented.

Weblink 5.1

Watch this YouTube video of students' application of *Gerbner's Cultivation Theory—Law & Order: SVU*: https://www.youtube.com/watch?v=gqvRKyrM1i4.

TELEVISION CRIME DRAMAS AND SECOND-ORDER CULTIVATION

The *CSI* Effect and Infotainment

Second-order cultivation (i.e., the attitudes developed from frequent media exposure) can take many forms. Recently, a widely contemplated example of television's influence has been identified as the *CSI* effect. The *CSI* effect is a largely unsupported belief commonly held by criminal justice officials, especially prosecutors, that because of the unrealistic scientific advancements used in crime solving on popular crime shows such as *CSI*, jurors are less likely to convict defendants if they are not presented with forensic evidence. The *CSI* effect portrays criminal justice as flawless. Dennis Stevens argues that the *CSI* effect is a result of popular media's success in portraying aggressive, reactive policing[7] as necessary, glorifying vigilantism, and portraying false accounts of crime and justice. Stevens notes that television media is very effective because people retain 50 percent of what they see and hear.[8]

We note that the *CSI* effect is largely unsupported because most research has not found evidence to support this belief.[9] However, there is a growing body of research that finds that prosecutors hold widely to this belief and have even begun to change the way they present their cases.[10] To further demonstrate this point, Garcia once served for three weeks as a juror in a criminal case. The case involved an attempted murder in which the prosecutor argued that the former boyfriend of a young woman was jealous of her current boyfriend and tried to kill him in a drive-by shooting. The problems that Garcia and the jury had with the case was the motive, placing the defendant (i.e., the accused) as the shooter, weighing contradictory testimony of a police officer, and the apparent racial concerns of the jury. The prosecution presented the jury with all types of photos and diagrams of the crime scene and the place where an altercation occurred prior to the shooting. He even required the jury to pass around the bloody bullet. If we ever doubted that prosecutors feared the *CSI* effect at work, Garcia's experience quickly quashed that thought. Garcia did not want to touch a bullet with dried blood on it with her bare hands; however, she was instructed that she was mandated under the law to examine the "evidence" in this manner. In this case, the prosecutor assumed that the forensic evidence would have greater weight than the fact that the elements of the case were not proven beyond a reasonable doubt.

The research shows that prosecutors and judges tend to believe that the *CSI* effect results in a large number of wrongful acquittals.[11] What we must consider in their beliefs is that it is not just *CSI*, but *CSI*-type shows. We must consider the *CSI* franchise. There is *CSI*, *CSI: Miami*, *CSI: NY*, and *CSI: Cyber*. These shows focus on the gathering of hard evidence and its forensic examination in order to solve criminal cases. You also can find many *CSI* spin-offs like the *NCIS* franchise, to include: *NCIS*, *NCIS: Los Angeles*, and *NCIS: New Orleans*. While these police procedurals place most of their focus on law enforcement investigations of the crimes, there is a strong emphasis on forensic evidence and its analysis. *Bones*, recently cancelled, takes another angle teaming a forensic expert with the FBI. *Rizzoli & Isles*, also recently cancelled, teams the medical examiner with law enforcement. In all of these police procedurals, the audience is told that crime can only be solved through scientific forensic examination of the evidence.

When examining jury decisions and the *CSI* effect, research has found that among mock jurors, *CSI* viewers were more likely to expect and have more knowledge of forensic evidence, but this rarely influenced their verdicts.[12] However, when one examines the frequency of viewing and perceived realism of these shows, then we find a *CSI* effect. In other words, jurors who frequently viewed *CSI*-type programs and who perceived those programs to be real were more likely to convict when there was forensic evidence. Thus, we see a validation of the criminal justice system that can be somewhat explained by police procedurals. Regardless, of the jurors' true understanding of science and forensics, police procedurals, which are created for entertainment purposes, appear to provide "information" to the audience.

Weblink 5.2

Listen to NPR's coverage of the *CSI* effect debate, "Is the 'CSI Effect' Influencing Courtrooms?": http://www.npr.org/2011/02/06/133497696/is-the-csi-effect-influencing-courtrooms.

Victims and Offenders

Second-order cultivation results in beliefs about victims and offenders as well as their relationships. In decades past, television crime dramas often focused on inner city crime and minority criminals. Police procedurals of the 1970s and 1980s, such as *CHiPs*, *Cagney & Lacey*, *Hawaii Five-O*, *Hill Street Blues*, *Kojak*, *Police Woman*, and *Starsky & Hutch*, typically portrayed victims as innocent, such as unsuspecting eye witnesses and fragile women, and as criminals who were caught on the opposite end of the crime. Television victims were also often police who were targeted by persistent superpredators. Victims were more likely than not to be white. Most criminals were frequently black, Italian, poor or financially desperate, and drug users. These police procedurals fit in line with common beliefs that victims are innocent white individuals and criminals are minority males and the worst people in society. Most people believe that criminals are young, poor, racial/ethnic minority males. The frequency of these images during these decades contributed to the re-enforcing spiral.

By the 1990s, crime dramas were not as rigid in their stereotypes of racial, ethnic, and economic minorities. One reason is because the media fail to hire many minority actors. In his research, Andrew Weaver tells us that producers fear that if they cast minorities as main characters then the viewers will define the programs as minority programs.[13] *Law & Order*, the first in the franchise, commonly portrayed victims and criminals as wealthy and often highly educated. *L.A. Law*, *Matlock*, and *Murder She Wrote*, three very popular crime dramas that aired from the mid-1980s to the mid-1990s also followed this narrative. Victims and offenders tended to be white, wealthy, and often somewhat powerful people.

The primary difference between the crime dramas of the 1990s and those of the 1970s and early 1980s was that they put more emphasis on the relationship between the victim and the offender. Previously, unless the victim was deviant in some way, he or she was usually a stranger to the offender. Beginning in the 1980s, more crime dramas portrayed a prior relationship between the victim and offender. Stranger danger was replaced with spouses, former intimate partners, and business partners.

Today's crime dramas have mostly continued with these victim and offender narratives. Programs like *Castle*, *NCIS*, *Bones*, and *Criminal Minds* tend to focus on wealthy criminals and victims but will slip in your occasional gangster who is typically Hispanic or black. However, a new type of crime drama has surfaced where the criminal is the focus. Crime dramas such as *Animal Kingdom*, *Breaking Bad*, *Better Call Saul*, *Dexter*, *Good Behavior*, *How to Get Away with Murder*, and *Mr. Robot*, among many others, frequently portray both victims and criminals as bad people. While society tends to see black males as the criminals of society, the only program in the previous list that features a black person as one of the main criminals is *How to Get Away with Murder*. Taking the criminal's point of view, the audience is presented with the bad-guy hero discussed in Chapter 4. As found in prior research by Andrew Weaver, it is possible that the shows' producers do not want their audiences to see the shows as "Black programs." In these programs, murder, drugs, and greed tend to be common episode plots, and victims are worse people than the criminal stars.

According to cultivation theory, the more exposure to these crime dramas, the more likely are viewers to internalize these stereotypes. Second-order cultivation would result in people believing that criminals are much more likely to be white wealthy males who had a prior relationship with their victims. However, we know that people still hold to the image of the symbolic assailant, that is, the young, violent, black male. However, if you recall our earlier discussion of the *CSI* effect, people who were frequent viewers of *CSI*-type programs and *who perceived those programs to be real* were more likely to convict defendants when there was forensic evidence. Perceived realism is a strong factor in determining what people take away from their television viewing. Those who watch crime dramas purely for entertainment are less likely to perceive that the programs portray reality. Also recall Jockel's and Fruh's discussion of moral foundation theory. People are drawn to programs that fit their morality. That morality binds individuals to see what they want to see and blinds them to other social facts that do not fit their moral foundation.[14] In this way, viewers may perceive parts of the program as a reflection of reality, such as the effectiveness of criminal justice, while rejecting as real the portrayal of the victims and offenders.

Weblink 5.3

For a discussion on moral foundation theory, go to: http://www.moral foundations.org/. This theory is not without its critics because it relies heavily on religion. It does, however, provide an interesting link to cultivation theory.

Offenders and Their Motives

When framing crime, the media often address motives. Within the news media, crime stories tend to be brief, following a formula of presentation. However, television and movie media are able to provide more detail, allowing the viewer to see the complexity of criminal behavior. Similar to news media, television series are constrained to a formula. The weekly program must be able to show the crime, the investigation that leads to the arrest of the offender, and provide solutions before the end of the hour. And like the selective internalization of images of victims and offenders, second-order cultivation within viewers tends to have a re-enforcing spiral binding and blinds viewers to beliefs they already hold strongly. Narratives of criminals' motives, like many others, follow a narrow set of stereotypes that viewers are comfortable with. Moving from series to series, episode to episode, viewers can find similar motives: anger or revenge, jealously, greed, emotional instability, mental pathology, and terrorism.

Following a television series formula, it is common to see jealousy as a common motive. In the jealousy narrative, the criminal is often a killer who commits the crime because he or she is jealous of the victim's romantic partner. In *CSI*'s "The Lost Girls" (S10, E7), Diane murders Deedee because Diane is jealous that Anthony, their pimp, likes Deedee more. In *Criminal Minds'* "Til Death Do Us Part" (S11, E3), Dana kills brides-to-be and then attempts to kill her sister Nicole who is engaged to the man she loves, Ryan. In this narrative, jealousy is linked to mental pathology or to anger. In so many of the jealousy narratives, we tend to find that women are far more likely to be portrayed as killing out of jealousy. Additionally, women are more likely to be portrayed as emotionally unstable. However, when we see a man killing out of jealousy, he is more likely to be portrayed as angry. In *Bones'* "Big in the Philippines" (S9, E13), bartender Joe Martucci kills country music artist Colin Haynes out of jealousy over a woman. In *NCIS*'s "Guilty Pleasure" (S7, E19), Navy Lieutenant Justin Moss is killed by a jealous boyfriend Dwight Kasdan. Kasdan was jealous of the Johns who hired his prostitute girlfriend.

The revenge narrative is often coupled with anger. Revenge crimes often reflect the perceived injustice the criminal has experienced. Theorist Robert Agnew argues that people are more likely to turn to crime when they perceive that an injustice has been done to them. Revenge as a motive for television crime dramas has become so common that the popular program *Revenge* aired for four seasons. In this show, Emily moves to the Hamptons in order to exact revenge on all of the people she believed wronged her father and family. In the previously discussed *NCIS* episode, Dwight Kasdan also kidnaps and attempts to murder the woman that he believes enticed his girlfriend into prostitution. Revenge is also frequently narrated when angry criminals attempt to bring down the police who arrested or injured them in some way. *NCIS*'s Agent Gibbs was kidnapped by the angry Reynosa drug cartel (S7, E24). Detective Rizzoli, of *Rizzoli & Isles*, was repeatedly victimized by Alice Sands who blamed Rizzoli for all of her problems. As with other motives, one can find an episode in every police procedural in which the police are victims of revenge.

Greed tends to be a motive in most economic crimes and many homicides. In crime dramas, the greed narrative often shows the criminal killing in order to keep wealth or to gain wealth that he or she believes is deserved. In *Castle*'s "Fool Me Once" (S1, E4), Sue kills her partner in crime, Fletcher, after he calls off the con of a wealthy woman he falls in love with. In *Law & Order*'s "Star Crossed" (S13, E14), Tina Montoya is able to seduce a mentally challenged young man, Robbie Delgado, into stealing for her. Her greed pushes her to manipulate people into giving her material things. Robbie even kills to impress her and then pleads guilty in order to protect her. Though not the only narrative, most greedy criminals in crime dramas are wealthy and white. Furthermore, while men are more likely to be portrayed as greedy, it is more common to portray greedy women as seductresses.

Mental pathology is a narrative that many crime dramas draw out in several episodes. More specifically, most series will bring out a story of a serial killer or two who tends to elude capture for some time. In *Bones*, serial killer Christopher Pelant stayed around for three seasons, while "The Ghost" took the show through several episodes. *NCIS* has had several serial killers as well but the one who really confused the team was the Port-to-Port Killer (PTP killer). Serial killers on television tend to be masterminds who play mind games with the police and evade capture time and again. They tend to be portrayed as calm, highly intelligent, and technological geniuses. They are also more likely to be males, unlike like The Ghost in *Bones*. In reality, there is a lot that we do not know about serial killers. Psychologists are still trying to understand what drives the different types of serial killers. Most do tend to be men. However, of the serial killers known to law enforcement, they tend not to be highly intelligent. Additionally, while the FBI has used many typologies, they have found that many serial killers are disorganized, acting spontaneously.[15]

Since 9/11, terrorism has been a popular narrative in most crime dramas, specifically police procedurals. However, crime dramas in which law enforcement is federal tend to be predominantly terrorism focused. *NCIS*, *NCIS: Los Angeles*, and *NCIS: New Orleans*, all have a strong terrorism focus, especially *NCIS: Law Angeles*. When *Castle*'s Detective Beckett took a position with the FBI, terrorism became a focus. Other crime dramas that center on terrorism include *24*, *Alias*, *Covert Affairs*, *Homeland*, *Person of Interest*, and *The Americans*. While many of the terrorists portrayed in these programs are of Middle Eastern decent, terrorists from other nations are also featured.

CULTIVATING CRIME IMAGES THROUGH TRUE-CRIME SERIES

Television true-crime series have been increasingly popular. This form of infotainment has also been called reality television and docudramas. Docudramas combine fiction and fact and tend to include reenactments. True-crime series give the appearance of objective reporting of true crimes. The presentation of the crimes using various camera angles and music typical in horror and action movies provides the entertainment the viewer is looking for.[16] Though there are so many, some of the more popular true-crime series include *America's Most Wanted*, *People vs. O.J. Simpson: American Crime Story*, *City Confidential*, *Cold Case Files*, *Cops*, *Dateline*, *Forensic Files*, *Gangland*, *True Crime with Aphrodite Jones*, *Snapped*, and *The First 48*. The crimes featured in these programs may take the audience through the criminal event or they may take the audience through the criminal's life.

As with crime news, police tend to be the gatekeepers in the information-processing system. These programs use a forensic journalism approach, telling the story mostly through the eyes of law enforcement. Many also include scenes of reenactments of the crime. The resulting second-order cultivation is the belief that the truth can only be provided when the investigating detectives, the prosecutors, and the victims' survivors tell the story. As the criminal is brought to light, we learn that greed, anger, and jealousy are the reasons for most crimes and that most crimes are very violent.

Examining the effects of true-crime series, we turn to the docudrama hypothesis that many researchers have adopted.[17] This hypothesis claims that when you combine fiction and documentary, people's conceptions of social and political reality are strongly influenced. Here the fiction tends to be the reenactments and the hard assumptions that the justice officials and victims' survivors are providing accurate information. Research has found that the viewing of docudramas is selective (i.e., selective exposure and selective avoidance). This results in the re-enforcing spiral. Again, we see the binding and blinding of one's preexisting belief systems. Sebastian Valenzuela and Angela Brandao argue that people are more likely to view programs that reinforce their belief systems and avoid those that negate them. This tends to increase polarization within society. In fact, we can see this polarization today in the many protests against police activities and political policies. Crime television tends to be conservative,[18] law and order-oriented, seeming accurate in its portrayal, and does not present strongly opposing viewpoints. As a result, people who spend more of their time viewing these programs tend to be more conservative.

True-Crime Series and Race

The way people of different races are portrayed in the media influences beliefs. While today African Americans are less likely to be portrayed as violent criminals in fictional programs, they are more likely to be portrayed as such in news and reality/true-crime programs.[19] Audiences are also more likely to see African Americans in custodial situations, such as handcuffed or behind bars. As we watch the program, we are told that the protectors of society, especially police, are almost always white.

Following the aforementioned knowledge, Mary Beth Oliver and G. Blake Armstrong examined viewing of the true-crime series, *Cops*, *American Detective*, *America's Most Wanted*, *Top Cops*, and *FBI: The Untold Story*. They found that the more people watched true-crime programs, the more likely were they to believe that crime is a bigger problem than is reality and that African Americans are more likely to be criminals. They also found that the viewers were more likely than not to perceive the programs to be realistic. In an earlier experiment, Oliver found that people who were authoritarian were more likely to enjoy viewing true-crime programs in which the police displayed aggression against criminal suspects but only if the suspect was black. Oliver and Armstrong also found that white viewers who enjoy true-crime programs, such as *Cops*, are more likely to display racial prejudice.

In many of the true-crime series, such as *City Confidential, Dateline,* and *Snapped,* we are more likely to see violent crimes committed by white middle-income or wealthy individuals. This is in direct contrast to cultural beliefs that racial and ethnic minorities, especially African Americans, are the vast majority of violent offenders. However, do not forget that producers tend to worry that a focus on black characters or, in this case, offenders, will label the series as a black program. The major difference between these true-crime series and those mentioned in the previous paragraph is that the former focus on street crimes. When true-crime series focus on crimes that occur off the streets, they are likely to focus on the "seemingly" quiet town or good girl or boy next door. These programs are more likely to present the case as shocking and an event that no one could have ever guessed would happen.[20] The second-order cultivation that results is that minorities are criminal, whites are justice officials, and if whites are criminals, then it is not a common occurrence.

True-Crime Series and Gender

The presentation of women and girls in society continues to follow gender role stereotypes. Within our gender role expectations, males are the protectors and the predators. Media reinforce these expectations by presenting males and females in stereotypical roles. We can see this in almost all of the true-crime series. With the exception of *Snapped,* which focuses only on female offending, criminals tend to be mostly men. These programs present images of male violence, cunning, and sometimes intelligence. Male crimes presented are more likely to involve gun violence.

The presentation of women and girls in society and the media reflects a disappointment or shock with the violent female who stepped out; that is, she stepped out of the gender role expectations that society dictates. Her criminal behavior is unfeminine and indicative of male aggression or an unstable woman. Eileen Berrington and Paivi Honkatukia explain that violent women are dichotomized (i.e., fit neatly into one of two categories).[21] They show how female killers are depicted by the media as either mad or bad. Since violence is defined to be unnatural for females, a female who kills must have something innately wrong with her. Serial killer Aileen Wuornos was portrayed as a psychopath, whose sexual orientation made her even more evil. Serial rapist and murderer Rosemary West was portrayed as an evil woman who lured her husband into her crimes. While male violence is portrayed as normal in that it is to be expected, female violence is demonized.[22] Deviation from traditional gender roles is depicted as evil, depraved, or pathological.

Box 5.1.   Female Criminals in Fictional Books

This book focuses on crime and justice in popular media. Much of these images are dictated by television ratings, box office profits, and media formulas and frames. However, while fictional books are written by single authors and not corporations, the factors that determine which types of books publishers will fund and release are based on the same factors that influence news, movie, and television media. Additionally, all are strongly influenced by social constructions of crime and justice. Similar to other portrayals, women's vulnerability, sexuality, and mental instability tends to be the major focus of women's criminality. Early crime fiction writers did not give much attention to criminal female characters as this was frowned upon.[23]

There have been, however, themes that have carried the image of the female criminal throughout time. The prostitute is a common theme. Inclusion of a female prostitute is frequently penned as a vulnerable and naïve woman who is economically exploited. Popular books about prostitutes have included *East of Eden* (1952), *Memoirs of a Geisha* (1997), and *The Lover* (2004).

A popular image is the poisoning woman. Historically, as midwives and housewives, women have had easy access to poisons and medicines. While women are no more likely to kill using poison than are men, this "quiet killing" is deemed to be more feminine. The poisoning woman was such a popular theme during the Victorian era that many literary critics feared the very theme would work to poison young women teaching them about crime and depravity.[24] Mary Elizabeth Braddon's books *The Trail of the Serpent* (1861) and *Barbara* (1880) were cited by the news media when covering murder trials of female poisoners.

Another theme in female criminality is the femme fatale or the black widow. The femme fatale seduces men and destroys their lives, figuratively or literally. From *The Maltese Falcon*'s (1930) Ruth Wonderly to *Gone Girl*'s (2012) Amy Dunne, women have frequently been portrayed as beguiling and dangerous, acting out of purely selfish or pathological reasons. As in the other forms of media, female criminals are often portrayed as mentally ill. Lisbeth Salander in *The Girl with the Dragon Tattoo* (2008) is a mentally unstable crime victim who turns to crime in revenge. The unfortunate fact is that we see these themes in the processing of female criminals in the criminal and juvenile justice systems as well.

Weblink 5.4

We do not address crime in books in our book beyond Box 5.1. However, visit The Kent State University Press: http://www.kentstateuniver sitypress.com/category/series/true_crime_hist/, to see a detailed listing of crime books covering well known crimes.

CONCLUSION

In 2016, the Bureau of Labor Statistics released the *American Time Use Survey Summary*. It was learned that in 2015, Americans spent on average 5.1 to 5.8 hours on leisure activities and they spend on average 2.8 hours watching television.[25] That is more time most people spend on household chores and childcare. This means that outside of work and school, most people dedicate a good portion of their day to consuming images about crime and justice, considering these are the most widely watched programs. When we consider this information, one can image the level of cultivation that occurs. Since police procedurals, which tend to reinforce the law-and-order ideology, are the most commonly viewed programs, we can suspect that the typical viewer is conservative and the re-enforcing spiral is hard at work. It does not matter that most crime does not come to the attention of the police and that police are only able to solve a portion of the crime they are aware of. The re-enforcing spiral convinces the viewer that crime is a serious problem that only the police can solve.

As we saw in Chapter 3 and our discussion of Sasson's framing, just as the news media maintain a strong crime-control focus, so do television media. Crime television can be very fun to watch. Many of us love to be able to "veg out" in front of the television and watch our favorite shows. With the ability to watch a whole season or series through venues such as Netflix in few sittings, we can set our minds to absorb the messages of crime television without much thought. If we perceive the programs we watch to have even a level of realism, then we become part of the problem of reinforcing damaging stereotypes and failed policies.

Chapter 6

Policing Crime

PRESENTING IMAGES
AND CONTROLLING KNOWLEDGE

For several decades now, the government, both federal and state, has been in a war on crime. This war also includes a war on drugs, a war on gang violence, and a war on terror. The most telling word in this discussion is "war." War assumes a known offender. It assumes a violent, even deadly, offender. And it assumes the need for soldiers and lethal weapons. In this war, the police are the crime fighters and the offenders are the enemy. It is important to understand that our belief system defines war as a zero-sum game. This means that we can win the war on crime through arrests and incarceration (i.e., locking them up). These activities, it is presumed, will remove the offenders and make society safe. The problem with this belief has been that the increase in arrests and people sent to prison has not made people feel safer. Although the crime rates have dramatically decreased since the declaration of this war, these activities have consistently been found to be unrelated to these decreases.[1] Additionally, the public, politicians, and law enforcement consistently cry for harsher handling of crimes and criminals.

Media have focused on this image of war and have presented the police as tough, unstoppable crime fighters. This is not to say that the police are always presented as the noble and good soldiers that society desires. The media also often focus on incompetence and corruption. However, in most portrayals, the forceful tactics used by the police are presented as necessary in the war on crime. We begin this chapter with a discussion on the history of police in the media. We then present media images of police in the war on crime, as well as issues of masculinity and race. Images of police as superheroes or corrupt cops within the movies and television police procedurals abound.

And one must never omit a discussion of police in the news and the recent concerns of police shootings. A popular theme has been the excessive and deadly use of force against African American males. While many of these events are obvious violations of civil rights, the increasing use of social media has helped to spread the tainted image to even the most competent and honest police officers. On the other hand, we still find that most police procedurals and true-crime programs still provide a positive image of law enforcement as dedicated experts working hard to fight crime.

THE HISTORY OF POLICE IN THE MEDIA

In Chapter 2, we discussed the fact that early crime news relied on witnesses and court personnel to provide facts about the crime. However, by the late 1800s, with the birth of yellow journalism, police became the new expert on crime facts. Police became the gatekeepers of the knowledge the public would learn about true crime. Although this was strongly influenced by the need to sell newspapers, it helped to create an image of the police as highly knowledgeable and competent in understanding the workings of crime and criminals. Today, the police still serve as the gatekeepers of crime. Although social media helps to bring issues of crime and justice to the media, the police still serve as the final word that validates what is real and factual.

Media images of police in the movies, however, began more as satire. As described by Ray Surette in *Media, Crime and Criminal Justice*,[2] early images presented police as bumbling, confused, incompetents who did not know which way to go. Surette describes these images as lampooned police. Silent comedy films of the early 1900s presented the Keystone Kops who often collided with each other in their failed attempts to capture the much smarter criminal. Today, most images of police have moved away from the Keystone Kops; however, we can see some of this in movies, along with their sequels, such as *Police Academy*, *Hot Shots*, *Naked Gun*, *Beverly Hills Cops*, *Super Trooper*, *21 Jump Street*, *22 Jump Street*, and *CHIPS*. Similarly, television media have engaged in its share of poking fun at police. Sitcoms such as *Angie Tribeca*, *Barney Miller*, *Brooklyn Nine-Nine*, *Car 54, Where Are You?*, and *The Andy Griffith Show* have portrayed police as incompetent, bumbling idiots. While early images reflected some truth of public views toward police, today's public is unlikely to perceive police as this incompetent.

Starting after the Great Depression, images of local police were muted and replaced with the G-man. Typically, before the 1930s, movies focused on idolizing criminals as heroes of a disorganized and harsh society. However, after the Association of Motion Picture Producers, Inc., the Motion Picture Producers, and the Distributors of America, Inc., adopted the Motion Picture

Figure 6.1. *The Thief Catcher,* **1914 with Charlie Chaplin (left). Keystone Studios. Photo in the public domain.**

Code, also known as the Hays Code, these images changed drastically. The president's Hays Commission criticized the movie industry for glorifying criminals, ridiculing law enforcement, and providing encouragement of immoral activities for would-be criminals. The movie industry, through the Hays Code, determined that it could become a force for improving society. The Hays Code generated the following general principles:

1 No picture shall be produced which will lower the moral standards of those who see it. Hence the sympathy of the audience should never be thrown to the side of crime, wrongdoing, evil, or sin.
2 Correct standards of life shall be presented on the screen, subject only to necessary dramatic contrasts.
3 Law, natural or human, should not be ridiculed, nor shall sympathy be created for its violation.[3]

The code, beginning in 1934, resulted in a wave of propaganda films[4] designed to portray federal law enforcement government agents, or G-men, as heroes fighting a never-ending battle against the violence of organized crime. The only way G-men were able to stop these violent criminals was through violence. Where the movies previously portrayed organized gangsters as heroes in an unforgiving society, the G-men became the heroes of society.

Local police, during the time of G-men were often portrayed as corrupt or incompetent. However, starting in the 1940s, police procedurals were introduced with television shows and movies such as *Dragnet*, and *Dick Tracy*.[5] According to Surette, police procedurals showed the workings of policing appearing as a docudrama. *Dragnet* always opened with the disclaimer that the events portrayed in the episode were true. This gave the impression that the audience was watching real-life policing. Within these shows, police were portrayed as very professional, focused, and committed to investigating crimes and arresting criminals. They were also portrayed as very successful in their efforts. Modern-day police procedurals include the *Law & Order* franchise, the *CSI* franchise, *The Wire*, *Major Crimes*, and the *NCIS* franchise.

Finally, in the 1970s, the media created an image of police as cops. This frame was launched with the movie *Dirty Harry* and the television show *Police Story*.[6] Similar to G-men, cops were faced with fighting a permanent crime war riddled with extremely violent offenders. Breaking from the G-men narrative, cops were handcuffed with criminal procedures such as probable cause, sufficient evidence, warrants, and other "pesky" due process rights and administrative red tape. The only way that cops were able to fight this losing war was by becoming vigilantes and aggressively engaging with criminals. Cops in these shows became increasingly paramilitary. Police procedurals such as *APB*, *Hawaii Five-O*, *Numbers*, *Castle*, and *NCIS: Los Angeles* show law enforcement frequently in gun battles, wearing bulletproof vests, and using modern technology. Movies fitting this description are plenty and include the *Lethal Weapon* and *Die Hard* franchises, *Bad Boys*, *End of Watch*, *The Departed*, and *Robocop*, to name just a few. However, as we will see, there are many cop frames in the war on crime, and news media are more likely to portray police in a negative light.

THE WAR ON CRIME

Police Soldiers

In 1965, President Lyndon B. Johnson declared a war on crime. At that time, crime was on the rise, though it did not peak until the mid-1990s. In his March 9, 1966 message to Congress, President Johnson, discussed a "unified attack" on crime that included an "immediate attack" and "comprehensive agenda" and "attacking crime at the roots."[7] In his proposal, Johnson stated that, "The front-line soldier in the war on crime is the local law enforcement officer."[8] He also stressed gun control; college education of police officers;

and technology improvement, such as police communications systems, developing computerized crime information systems, and increasing police equipment. While the additional points could be used to accomplish a professional peacekeeping police organization, the emphasis was the attack on crime. So the war began and the media ran with it.

Our images of war and soldiers allow for an increased level of violence that police as peacekeepers are not awarded. In a very intelligent article on the depiction of the war on crime in Baltimore, Philip Joseph analyzes HBO's police procedural *The Wire*. In his analysis of this police procedural, the war on crime in the City of Baltimore was equated to the *new war*.[9] In the new war, as described by Joseph and other scholars, there is asymmetry of the players. This means that the police who represent the state are well trained and well equipped, while the enemies are the criminals, even the noncriminal residents, who are nonstate and not very well organized. The city becomes the war zone because the state has failed to keep control and protect the civilians. The state must then become militarized as the people within the city still count on this failed state to protect them. The police become soldiers using militarized tactics against their enemy.

In his analysis, Joseph describes a scene in the first episode where an officer is complaining that you cannot even call it a war because wars end. *The Wire* opens with the message that the war on crime is worse than a traditional war. *The Wire*, according to Joseph, shows that the state, this includes the police, has created conditions that force youth to turn to crime in order to survive. If you recall Sasson's frames, this shows the faulty system frame. The faulty system leads to untold crime which then requires the police to go to war with criminals. While the show makes it a point to show that blame lies largely on the government and the police, it also stresses the need to control crime by any means necessary.

Campbell and Campbell argue that police officers are increasingly becoming soldiers and soldiers are taking on policing roles.[10] We see an increase in police paramiliatary units (PPU or S.W.A.T.) teams, as well as "greater use of collective force, heavier weapons, full ballistic gear, aggressive patrol work, and no-knock warrants."[11] On primetime television, we can see this in police procedurals such as *APB*, *Hawaii Five-O*, *NCIS*, *Southland*, and *The Wire*, to name a few. Additionally, even police procedurals that focus on science and police investigative skills often include S.W.A.T. scenes, shootouts, and other intense scenes when the police have to draw their guns. Crime movies are much more likely to involve extreme violence analogous to war scenes. Even the very popular *Fast and Furious* franchise joins the war on crime when in *Furious 7*, the team of outlaws is approached by a secret federal government agency and is asked to take down a cyberterrorist. The message in the movie is that the war on crime requires a level violence and maneuvering that is illegal. The movie is riddled with explosions, combat helicopters, and flying cars. The *Bad Boys* of Florida were fighting a war on drugs that brings the bullets into their personal lives and even requires them to sneak into other countries.

However, the entertainment media are not the only ones holding strongly to the war on crime and police as soldiers. Since 9/11, the image of police as soldiers in a war against terror on the homeland has increased. Of particular focus has been police response to civil disobedience and public protests. Protestors in the wake of the police shooting of eighteen-year-old Michael Brown were met with a militarized police force (see Box 6.1). Some of the more well-publicized protests covered in the news, which included a focus of a militarized police include: the 2017 Presidential Inauguration of Donald Trump in Washington, D.C.; the demonstration at the 2016 California GOP Convention; the Occupy Wall Street protests; the Black Lives Matter protests, the 1999 Seattle World Trade Organization protests, and the 2004 protest of the Republican Convention in New York.

Weblink 6.1

Visit the U.S. National Library of Medicine's National Center for Biotechnology Information to read about Professor Hannah L. F. Cooper's research on "War on Drugs Policing and Police Brutality": https://www. ncbi.nlm.nih.gov/pmc/articles/PMC4800748/.

Box 6.1.   A Militarized Police in the Face of Civil Rights Protests

In the war on crime, in addition to defining criminals as enemy combatants, the police will often treat people engaging in protests and civil disobedience as enemy combatants. This was made apparent with the protestors of the police shooting of Michael Brown in Ferguson, Missouri. On August 9, 2014, unarmed eighteen-year-old Michael Brown was shot and killed by Ferguson Police Officer Darren Wilson, a white man.[12] In the aftermath of a grand jury failing to indict Officer Wilson (i.e., they did not charge him with a crime), a peaceful protest was scheduled to occur in the streets of Ferguson. This was yet another protest in the Black Lives Matter movement. However, the nation was shocked when the news media broadcast photos and videos of protestors being met by police with military equipment. The protest soon broke out in violence. Though most of the protestors were nonviolent, the news stories kept their focus on the violent youth. Soon a protester was shot by police, buildings were set on fire, and stores were looted. After a state of emergency was called and ended, a federal investigation was conducted. The U.S. Department of Justice found that the police department discriminated against African Americans and later a consent decree required that the department undergo changes in police training and procedure, wear body cameras, and be subject to civilian oversight.

Figure 6.2.   Police in riot gear. Photo courtesy of Pexels.

Weblink 6.2

The Movement for Black Lives is a consortium of more than fifty organizations active in the Black Lives Matter movement. Visit their website to learn more about the people's demands: https://policy.m4bl.org/.

Crime Scene Investigators

In our war on crime, training police soldiers is not enough. The average police officer in the United States has some higher education. Just over half of police departments reimburse some college tuition and some departments will put efforts into recruiting from colleges (14 percent).[13] Most police departments within the nation are located in suburban and rural jurisdictions. These agencies are located within communities with lower crime rates and where police do not have the experience or resources to solve very complicated crimes. Sometimes the police need expert help in the way of forensic science in order to solve crimes. These experts are typically the crime scene investigators (CSIs). Similar to the way news media engages in forensic journalism, television often relies on forensics, albeit scientific experts, to solve crimes. News and movies do not place emphasis on CSIs; however, television police procedurals have run with the CSI concept since 2000.

Imagine that a gruesome murder has taken place. The police arrive at the scene but have no leads as murderers do not typically stick around and confess. What are the police to do? They call in CSIs, and these scientific investigators gather up every piece of evidence on the scene. The CSIs can eyeball a footprint and identify the size and shoemaker. They can see a tire tread mark and know the make and model, even the year, of the car. Tiny pieces of glass shards found on the busy street of the murder scene are always linked to the murder. And DNA is almost always found. So what do the CSIs do? They take whatever evidence they can find back to the lab. Whatever evidence that has not already been analyzed and confirmed on the scene is analyzed in the lab. The mass spectrometer, pH tester, forensic swab dyer, borescope, POW-DERado SH131, Ninhydrin, DFO, and Indandione Fingerprint Development Chamber, UV-Box decontamination chamber, CRU Wiebe Tech USB 3.0 WriteBlocker, and the M-Vac forensic DNA collection system, to name but a few forensic tools, are all put to use back in the crime lab. Within a few hours, okay sometimes a couple of days, the CSI experts have analyzed all of the evidence, determined how the crime was committed, why the crime was committed, and who committed the crime. The police are only there to pick up the offender and get a confession. But really, who needs a confession when the evidence speaks for itself.

These CSIs and their capabilities are amazing; they are also a fantasy, or rather a television fantasy. *CSI: Crime Scene Investigation* was the first police procedural to run with this fairy tale of forensics experts who can identity every piece of evidence at every scene in very short time spans in order to solve crimes. From Nick Stokes to Catherine Willows to Coroner Al Robbins to numerous other scientists, *CSI* aired from 2000 to 2015, with spinoffs, *CSI: NY*, *CSI: Miami*, and *CSI: Cyber*, solving countless crimes that would never be solved but for the science. So popular were these shows that other *CSI*-type shows soon surfaced. *NCIS* has forensic scientist Abby Sciuto, Dr. Donald "Ducky" Mallard, and Dr. Jimmy Palmer. *Bones* has Dr. Temperance Brennan and her staff at the Smithsonian. *Rizzoli & Isles* has Coroner Dr. Maura Isles, and so on. These doctors and scientists can uncover the unknown and solve the unsolvable. The extent of their knowledge is endless.

Unfortunately, these situations are unrealistic. Most police departments do not have crime labs at their disposal. Most police departments rely solely on the coroner to pronounce the time and cause of death but do not have highly trained CSIs at their disposal. In most cases, the police must send their evidence to crime labs located in another part of the state. At that point, the evidence is logged in and backlogged. The latest census of publicly funded forensic crime labs (those used by the police) found that, in 2014, there were 3.8 million requests for forensic analyses for the 409 crime labs.[14] The labs had a backlog of 570,100 requests. This means that about 16 percent of all requests are not completed within thirty days. Between 30 percent and 40 percent of all lab requests are for DNA, and over 64,000, or 11 percent, of the backlog were requests for DNA analysis.

DNA is a major focus in solving crimes. Since 1992, The Innocence Project has helped to exonerate 349 inmates through DNA testing.[15] DNA evidence has been determined to be the most reliable form of evidence and was first introduced into the court in the mid-1980s. However, DNA evidence was not commonly allowed into the court room until relatively recently and most CSIs do not collect DNA evidence. DNA evidence can take over two days to extract and analyze. However, considering the many departmental requests to the very few crime labs, this tends to take much longer. Yet, in police procedurals the lab scientists are able to finish the task within a few hours and within a few days the entire case is solved. Who needs police? CSIs are the modern-day police.

Weblink 6.3

Learn about The Forensic Chemistry Lab/Instrument at the University at Albany's Department of Chemistry. Go to: http://www.albany.edu/chemistry/forensicIntrumentation.shtml.

Amateur Sleuths and Private Detectives

If CSIs do not appeal to you, you can find many television programs and movies in which the amateur sleuth or private detective solves the crime. Just like the CSIs, unofficial good-guy heroes who are amateur sleuths and private detectives are portrayed as needed in the war on crime. In some crime dramas, the police need a special private detective to do what they do not have the time, resources, or expertise to do. Television's *Perception*, tells the story of the FBI who must rely on amateur sleuth and neuropsychiatrist Dr. Daniel Pierce to solve the most difficult cases. A few years before *Perception, Monk,* a detective consultant, aided the police in solving difficult cases. In both of these police procedurals, these private citizens were brilliant individuals whose mental disabilities allowed them to see the minutest details.

Sherlock Holmes is the most famous sleuth. His brilliance makes the police appear incompetent. Over the years, the character of Holmes has jumped from the pages of Sir Arthur Conan Doyle to the big screen and the television. In Chapter 4, we analyzed the framing of *Sherlock Holmes*. We also see his character in television's *Elementary* and the United Kingdom's *Sherlock*. With his brilliance and pomposity, Sherlock Holmes makes it clear that he is the only one who can solve difficult crimes. Other such amateur detectives on television who solve crimes the police cannot fathom include *Psych*, *Veronica Mars*, *Lie to Me*, *The Mentalist*, even serial killer *Dexter* plays the amateur sleuth.

In the past several years, we have seen a resurgence of a crime genre that has recently been labeled "cozy mysteries." Initially found in the books of authors like Agatha Christie and Janet Evanovich, cozy mysteries have been made into movies on television and occasionally on the big screen. Cozy mysteries are stories written by women about female amateur sleuths who step out of the traditional feminine gender role and through persistence manage to solve murders that stump the police.[16] Often the female amateur sleuth sees a murder where the police do not. Then she persistently searches for clues bringing them to the police for consideration. The police often brush off the female sleuth as a bored meddling woman and warn her of the dangers of her actions. However, she persists, because she is intelligent and perceptive, until she solves the case.

The earliest long lasting series was *Murder She Wrote*. Between 1984 and 1996, mystery writer Jessica Fletcher, played by Angela Lansbury, solved murders on a weekly basis. Recently, however, the Hallmark Movies and Mysteries Channel© has released several cozy mysteries. In Charlaine Harris's *Aurora Teagarden* series,[17] Aurora is a librarian and president of a murder mystery book club who consistently finds herself in the middle of a murder. And while the police are hostile to her nosy activities, she always sees the clues that the police dismiss. In the *Murder She Baked* movies, Hannah Swenson is a baker who solves murders while delivering her amazing baked goods. The *Garage Sale Mystery* movies feature antique shop owner Jennifer Shannon who typically uncovers and solves murders as she searches garage and estate sales for hidden antiques. The *Flower Shop Mystery* movies and *Concrete Evidence* movies follow similar storylines. While, *Concrete Evidence*'s Shannon Hughes and *Hailey Dean* do not engage in traditional women's work, all of these movies tend to minimize official police involvement and avoid extreme violence and gore.

Weblink 6.4

Visit Cozy Mystery List for a detailed list of cozy mystery books, television programs, and movies: http://www.cozy-mystery.com/.

POLICE AND MASCULINITY

Women Police and Crime Fighters in the Media

No matter how involved the amateur sleuths and CSI experts become in solving crimes, using science, their uncommon intelligence and perception, or their inquisitive nature, the criminal justice system and the media have made it very clear that fighting crime is man's work. In 1905, Lola Baldwin was the first woman hired as a "safety worker;" she had arrest powers.[18] By the 1920s, 210 police departments employed 417 policewomen. By the 1960s, there were over 5,000 policewomen in the United States. However, because women were viewed to be too weak, emotional, and generally unfit to do police work, they were typically assigned to patrol duties, and most only worked with wayward women and children. In the 1970s, women represented only 3 percent of police personnel. By 2008, women represented 4,000 state police; 19,400 sheriffs' officers; 55,300 local police officers; and 18,200 federal officers.[19] Today, women comprise as much as 25 percent of federal law enforcement officers. And though that is not much, the images of law enforcement remain overwhelmingly male and masculine.

A quick Google search of the best police movies yields only two movies in which the starring law enforcement officer is a female: *Silence of the Lambs* and *Fargo*. In both of these movies, the female officer is portrayed in a gendered light. She is not masculine, quick to draw a gun, or quick to fight the bad guys. She uses communication skills instead of fighting skills. It seems that, similar to race, producers want to avoid having their movies labeled as "chick flicks." The one hundred top grossing U.S. crime movies, which include all crime genres, reveal that most of the crime-fighting stars are men.[20] There are eleven movies in this list with leading or supporting women in law enforcement (see table 6.1).

Data on top grossing crime movies are significant in that they tell us that movies with leading female crime fighters do not draw as large an audience. The top grossing movie with a female crime fighter in a major role grossed $144.73 million. The top grossing movie in which the star is a male crime fighter grossed $533.32 million (*The Dark Knight*). When we consider the movies with leading female crime fighters only six of the eleven have the females as the star. In the top movie, *Lethal Weapon 3*, Sergeant Lorna Cole,

Table 6.1.   Top Grossing U.S. Crime Titles with Leading/Supporting Female Crime Fighters

Movie Title and Rank	Dollars in the Millions
31. *Lethal Weapon 3*	144.73
38. *Bad Boys II*	138.40
47. *Silence of the Lambs*	130.73
49. *Lethal Weapon 4*	129.73
54. *Charlie's Angels*	125.31
59. *Salt*	118.31
66. *S.W.A.T.*	116.64
70. *Spy*	110.82
75. *Miss Congeniality*	106.81
88. *Charlie's Angels: Full Throttle*	100.69
100. *RED*	90.36

Note: *Signifies that the officer was the leading crime fighter.

is tough with superb fighting skills and can take a punch and a bullet. She is also the love interest of the supercop Martin Riggs. In its sequel *Lethal Weapon 4*, Sergeant Cole is pregnant throughout the entire movie. Playing a much smaller role, she longs to marry Detective Riggs.

In *Bad Boys II*, DEA Agent Syd Burnett is the sister of Detective Marcus Burnett and the girlfriend of Detective Mike Lowrey. Syd uses her intellect and sexuality to catch the bad guys but ultimately needs rescuing by the bad boy detectives. *Charlie's Angels* and *Charlie's Angels: Full Throttle* center on three beautiful female detectives who, though they are more than physically capable, rely on their sexuality to fight crime. They dress provocatively and often act empty-headed in order to get the job done. *Miss Congeniality*'s FBI Gracie Hart, starts as a masculine no-nonsense agent who knows nothing about being a "woman." However, the majority of the movie focuses on her undercover gig as a Miss United States beauty pageant contestant. The message here is that women in law enforcement are not real women until they learn to become real women, but then they fall in love and lose sight of the job.

Often the lead female star does not exhibit masculine traits of the tough, fighting protector of the innocent. FBI cadet Clarice Starling, the lead law enforcement character but co-star in *Silence of the Lambs*, uses intellect not physical prowess to obtain information from a serial killer. CIA analyst-turned-agent Susan Cooper bumbles her way through solving the case in *Spy*. Her covers focus on Cooper as a mother and a cat lady. As she breaks out of her assigned covers, she reinvents herself as a trendy female bodyguard. And although she possesses incredible fighting skills, she is often an accidental champion. Furthermore, she is driven by the belief that the man she loves was murdered by her target.

CIA Agent Evelyn Salt (*Salt*) is the only leading actress who plays a crime fighter and is a tough supercop. *Salt* is an action movie that rivals those starring male crime fighters. However, much of Agent Salt's drive is revenge for the murder of the man she loves. *S.W.A.T.*'s female officer, Chris Sanchez, is the most masculine female crime fighter in the top one hundred grossing movies in the United States. She is tough, no-nonsense, and can beat up most men. She walks tough, speaks tough, and has a man's name. She also has a child and has to find a babysitter in order to stay out late. She also is a supporting actress in the movie. Finally, Victoria (*RED*), a former British Agent, is a gun-toting "bad ass." Her character is very feminine, dainty, and proper. While she can cold-heartedly kill as well as the next male crime fighter, she never breaks a sweat or a nail. Her story centers on her love of former Russian Agent Ivan Simanov.

Similarly, the highest-rated television police procedurals star male crime fighters. As discussed in Chapter 5, four of the top ten primetime broadcast network shows for 2016 were crime shows, mostly police procedurals (*NCIS*, *Bull*, *NCIS: New Orleans*, and *Blue Bloods*). None of these programs starred a female crime fighter. Other popular police procedurals that had a female crime fighter as the lead are *Bones*, *Castle*, *Cold Case*, *Homeland*, *Major Crimes*, *Marvel's Agent Carter*, *Quantico*, *Rizzoli & Isles*, *Sleepy Hollow*, and *The Closer*. Unlike crime movies, most television cops are not supercops and the programs contain a lot of drama. However, we find that police procedurals in which women are the lead officers tend to be lighter and focus on intimate relationships more. The female leads in *Bones*, *Castle*, *Major Crimes*, and *The Closer* married or became engaged with male main characters. *Marvel's Agent Carter* pined over her long-lost love, as did Detective Rizzoli in *Rizzoli & Isles*. While *Homeland* does not focus on her romantic entanglements, she was previously romantically involved with her boss. Furthermore, similar to the stereotype of female criminals, CIA Agent Carrie Mathison is mentally unstable.

Weblink 6.5

To learn more about women in policing at the National Center for Women & Policing, visit: http://womenandpolicing.com.

Masculinity and the Supercop

Policing has always been a male-dominated field. The role of the police is to protect the people from criminals. As such, it is deemed "man's work." Just as "woman's work" of child-rearing requires patience and nurturing qualities, man's work requires strength, intelligence, physical agility, and a good amount of risk-taking. These are traditional gender roles that most boys are still socialized into when they are young. It makes them good protectors and good providers of the family. Since traditional gender role socialization does not raise girls in the same light, their movement into policing was largely rejected.[21] As discussed earlier, women's movement into law enforcement has increased, however, so has the masculinization of law enforcement. As seen in Box 6.1, police are increasingly readopting a paramilitary or, some would argue, a military configuration. The war on crime requires soldiers that are much more strongly aligned with masculinity.

First, we start with visual images. A quick news search on Google using terms such as police, police officer, law enforcement, and arrest yields over 22 million stories. Accompanying pictures include mug shots; crime scenes; victims; officers; and crime-fighting symbols such as cars, yellow crime scene tape, and government buildings. Of course, we did not go through all 22 million stories. However, a quick browse of the first eight pages for each search term resulted in one picture of a female officer who was paralyzed in the line of duty. A news search for police equipment yields pictures of police badges, police guns, police cars, police shields, helmets, bulletproof vests, handcuffs, bomb dismantling equipment, police drones, and police dogs. In the first eight pages of the 22,900,000 hits of this news search, there was one gavel (a symbol of justice and the courts), one data chart, one picture of surveillance equipment in a case, and no images of women in the pictures.

This information is relevant because the visuals portrayed by the media supports the idea that we are in a war on crime fought by male soldiers. These images do not reveal the 80–20 rule.[22] That is, as a rule for most police departments, 80 percent of police work involves social work-type activities, such as community policing, community outreach, simple and uneventful patrolling, and settling minor disputes. On the other end, 20 percent of police work involves crime fighting, but not the type of fighting found in action movies. Spending too much time watching police procedurals and crime movies, people often believe that the opposite is true. When she first started teaching, Dr. Garcia was approached by a student who informed her that he wanted to be a police officer because he wanted to see action. She tried explaining over and over the 80–20 rule; however, the student was not convinced. This has been a frequent conversation with students for the past twenty-three years of teaching. Students want the excitement they see in the news when police respond to bomb threats and protests alike, in military gear.

Nowhere does the media scream masculinity than on the big screen. In Chapter 4, we discussed crime in the movies. Of the ten top grossing U.S. crime movies we analyzed, half of them were action crime movies. This meant lots of great explosions, car chases, and gun fights. The fun part about these movies is that the crime fighting heroes are unstoppable superheroes, or supercops. In *Bad Boys II*, the detectives' motto was "we ride together, we die together, Bad Boys for life." This motto is the ultimate expression of the unstoppable masculine soldier in the war on crime. The *Bad Boys* of Florida had military equipment at their fingertips, and while they did not have military training they worked with officers who did. Additionally, in the war on crime, with the unspoken permission of their commanding supervisor, they were forced to travel to Cuba in order to save the damsel in distress, a female DEA agent.

Superhero crime fighters were also displayed in *Sherlock Holmes* in which highly intelligent private detectives were able to escape explosions, bullets, and extremely large bad guys. In *Taken 2*, it takes a retired CIA agent, the stereotype of the supercop, to rescue his kidnapped ex-wife. And *Furious 7* faced such dangerous terrorists that the government was forced to turn to daredevils to save society. The images of the supercop abound and when the crime fighter is not a police officer then the world must turn to the private citizen superhero. Among the top grossing U.S. crime movies, twenty of the top fifty were crime-fighting movies that involved mostly male superheroes or supercops. Garcia and Arkerson are highly entertained by these movies, especially by the explosions. Unfortunately, many people view these movies holding a level of perceived realism.

Weblink 6.6

Read a blog in *The Huffington Post* on "The Police and Their Masculinity Problem" at: http://www.huffingtonpost.com/myisha-cherry/the-police-and-their-masc_b_6225834.html.

GOOD COPS—BAD COPS

In the war on crime, sometimes the police must fight themselves. There is no shortage of bad cop movies. One of the most popular and loved bad cop movies is *Training Day*. The movie's veteran Detective Alonzo Harris (played by the famous Denzel Washington), is a corrupt cop who tries to train his rookie partner, Officer Jake Hoyt. Detective Harris is quick to learn that Officer Hoyt is incorruptible and the movie becomes a war of good cop versus bad cop. Many other corrupt cop movies have been produced over the years, such as *Cop Land, L.A. Confidential, Lakeview Terrace, No Rest for the Wicked, The Departed*, and *The Untouchables,* to name just a few. However, in most of the corrupt cop movies, you will find good cops fighting hard to obtain justice, such as in *Crash*, *Dirty Harry*, *Four Brothers*, *Training Day*, and *Serpico*. In other cases, the corrupt cop confronts himself and tries to atone for his sins. Some of these movies include *Cop Land*, *Bad Lieutenant*, *Gangster Squad*, *L.A. Confidential*, *Dark Blue*, and *Mulholland Falls*. These bad cops-turned-hero have always been popular because they return us to our moral comfort.[23] Popular police procedurals with corrupt cops include *Gotham*, *Justified*, *Low Winter Sun*, *Sons of Anarchy*, *The Shield, The Wire*, and *Boardwalk Empire*, and one cannot forget the popular 1980s program *The Dukes of Hazzard*. Good cop movies tend to feature the superhero and draw in large audiences at the box office. However, many of the corrupt cop movies involve bad cops-turned-good and thus are viewed as criminal heroes, or bad-good guys.

Police and Race

Race is often taken for granted in television and movie depictions of police. Typically, police are white, male actors (unless it is a minority program)[24] and minorities are more likely to be cast as suspects and criminals. However, race tends to be a central focus in the news. Of particular focus are the police–African American community relations. It is well known that police have been at the forefront in the oppression of African Americans in our society, both historically and currently.[25] The mistreatment of minorities, and especially African American males, has been a focus of much of the criminological research. One outcome has been the lack of trust and confidence in the police by minorities.[26] However, we must understand that direct and historical contact and mistreatment by police is not the only factor that influences public trust and confidence. Research has found that news coverage of police corruption can have both national and local negative impact on public trust and confidence.[27]

Police shootings of African American males is one of the main problems identified by today's news media and by advocates of civil rights. From recent research, we know that police are more likely to use deadly force against minorities. Armed as well as unarmed black and Hispanic males are more likely to be shot than are white males.[28] Additionally, in 2015, *The Washington Post* started to track the fatal police shootings reported in the media.[29] Since January 1, 2015, the media have reported that 2,243 people have been shot and killed by the police. Thus far, news reports have identified that blacks are overrepresented in fatal shootings, even when unarmed. The tracking of police shootings was, in part, a response to public outcry and the Black Lives Matter movement.

#BlackLivesMatters was created in the aftermath of the 2012 murder of unarmed seventeen-year-old Trayvon Martin by George Zimmerman (see Weblink 1.1). Zimmerman, a civilian, was acting on the belief that Trayvon, a black youth wearing a hood, was a suspicious person. He followed Trayvon with a gun and ultimately shot and killed him. Zimmerman was not arrested until public outcry over the event and ultimately he was not convicted of the crime. The hashtag was created as a social media forum in response to Zimmerman's acquittal. However, following the police killings of other black males, Black Lives Matter became the campaign used by protestors. The police killings of many black males in the past few years have been met with angry and mostly peaceful protests. With these events, news coverage often begins with the telling of the killing, questioning the police and alluding to outright or implicit racism. It is common for news stories to stress that yet another white officer has killed yet another black man. However, the stories often quickly turn to the victim's deviance or criminal behavior at any point in his life. This is typical because the police are the trusted gatekeepers of the media and engage in image management.[30] The news stories then move to the protestors, who start peaceful, and often portray the police in a critical light. However, once there is any protestor violence and violent police pushback, the news tends to move back in favor of police tactics.

Largely influenced by the Black Lives Matter movement, police accountability has also become a central focus of the media. Accountability today is largely equated with surveillance by way of body cameras and consent decrees. A Google news search yields 1,420,000 police accountability and 711,000 body cameras stories. Reports on public demands helped to push local governments to fund body cameras programs. However, we still find that most of the news stories of excessive use of force are uncovered by private citizen videos. Consent decrees have also become a focus of the news media, with 45,300 stories in a Google news search. As of April 2015, fourteen police departments were under consent decrees with mandates to correct problems of discrimination. The largest of these departments include Miami, Newark, Cleveland, Ferguson, Baltimore, Seattle, New Orleans, and Chicago.[31] However, the biggest news reporting at the time this book was written was the concern that the Trump administration would dismantle the federal practice of consent decrees that has pushed police reform.[32] If this move is achieved, it is possible that we may see an increased social construction of police in the news as bad cops.

Weblink 6.7

For a detailed description of how police are expected to behave, read the *Final Report to the International Association of Chiefs of Police by the Administration of Justice Reform George Mason University* at: http://www.iacp.org/The-Public-Image-of-the-Police#ch4.

CONCLUSION

For all of its focus on crime and the ineffectiveness of justice, the media still overwhelming provide a positive image of the police. While we may see movies of vigilante and corrupt cops, we are more likely to see most of these cops either taken down by hero police or changing their ways. Television may display the occasional corrupt officer; however, images of police heroes abound. And news media may dedicate a good portion of its crime coverage to police corruption and discrimination; however, it puts far more effort into covering the crime-fighting activities of the police. Together, media cultivate a very positive image of the police. First-order cultivation creates the perception that the police are the good soldiers in our war on crime. Second-order cultivation creates beliefs that while there are a few bad apples in the police tree, most officers who use violence use what is necessary to take down very dangerous criminals. In this law-and-order era, people are still more than likely to support police militarization and the use of violence.

Chapter 7

Courtrooms and Lawyers in the Media

WHERE HAVE ALL OF THE LEGAL PROCEDURALS GONE?

Where crime and police are an all-time favorite of the media, the courts and corrections have nearly disappeared. Even the well-loved *Law & Order* television legal procedural has ended. *Law & Order* dedicates the first half of each episode to investigating the crime and the other half to prosecuting it. *Law & Order* spin-offs, such as *Law & Order: Special Victims Unit* and *Law & Order: Criminal Intent*, place minimal focus on prosecution and the courts, reflecting the strict police procedural. Gone are the popular courtroom dramas and legal procedurals, such as *Ally McBeal*, *Boston Legal*, *JAG*, *L.A. Law*, *Matlock*, and *Perry Mason*. Recent attempts to revive legal procedurals have not been as successful. *Franklin & Bash* only lasted four seasons. *Conviction*, a legal procedural about lawyers who investigate the integrity of old convictions, only lasted for one season. However, *Chicago Justice* and *Bull* are more recent legal procedurals that were doing well at the time this book was written.

There have been many movie courtroom dramas. Famous courtroom dramas include *Judgement at Nuremburg*, *To Kill a Mockingbird*, *A Few Good Men*, and *Philadelphia*. Richard Brust published "The 25 Greatest Legal Movies" in the *American Bar Association Journal* (*ABA Journal*).[1] These movies represented eighty-five Oscar nominations and thirty-one Oscar wins. According to twelve prominent lawyers, the five best legal movies are *To Kill a Mockingbird*, *12 Angry Men*, *My Cousin Vinny*, *Anatomy of a Murder*, and *Inherit the Wind*. Only two of the top twenty identified by Brust were released in the 2000s and eight in the 1990s. The AMC Filmsite tracks movies by genre, Oscars, and highest grossing among many other factors.[2] Only one courtroom drama made the list of the all-time highest grossing films, *A*

Few Good Men. We know that drama does not sell as much as action. But what social constructs are being sold to us?

THE PROSECUTION VERSUS THE DEFENSE

Prosecutors and defense attorneys are not fodder for blockbuster sales nor do they take up much television air time, especially primetime. Television legal procedurals tend to place more focus on interpersonal relationships than they do on fighting crime and seeking justice. Where police are fighting crime, lawyers are fighting the law. Where police are struggling through intimate relationships or not experiencing any, lawyers are exploring intimate relationships and developing strong friendships with coworkers. Television legal procedurals are dramas, while most legal movies today tend to be thrillers. The focus of many courtroom dramas/legal movies is on revealing the villain either in the courtroom or on the streets. We refer to most movies here as lawyer or legal movies instead of the more commonly used name courtroom drama. In the courtroom drama, a large amount of time is given to the inner workings of the court. The audience is given a bird's-eye view of opening statements and litigation in the courtroom. They even include legal research into the cases. Lawyer movies tend to focus on the lawyer and the lawyer's struggles.

In most of the top grossing legal movies, the lawyer is a defense attorney. While social constructs place the defense attorney in the same light as the criminal, most lawyer movies portray them as noble. The most famous movie in the previously mentioned list, *To Kill a Mockingbird*, paints defense attorney, Atticus Finch, as a moral advocate who is willing to put his life and reputation on the line to ensure that the truth is told and justice is served.[3] *A Time to Kill* follows the same formula but also includes violence to draw in the audience.

The conflict within lawyer movies is the adversarial nature of criminal justice. The defense counsel struggles to ensure that the defendant's rights are upheld, while the prosecutor, who represents law enforcement, fights to ensure that crime does not pay. The excitement is in the courtroom drama. Lawyers provide eloquent and captivating opening and closing statements. They come close to badgering a witness in hopes of confusing them into a confession; and this almost always happens while on the stand. In the courtroom drama, the excitement is in the objections made by the opposing attorney. In the lawyer movie, the excitement is in the out-of-court struggles, sometimes violent, in trying to investigate the crime.

Thane Rosenbaum describes six types of lawyer movies.[4] These include the heroic lawyer, the obtuse lawyer, the disillusioned lawyer, the vengeful lawyer, horror lawyer movies, and comedy lawyer movies. The heroic lawyer, the obtuse lawyer, and the disillusioned lawyer are the most common in the movies and can be seen in most legal procedurals. The heroic lawyer is very noble and may even put the legal system on trial. Atticus Finch points out the injustice of a racialized legal system, as does *A Time to Kill*'s defense attorney Jake Tyler Brigance. Television's defense attorney *Perry Mason* and *Law & Order*'s prosecutor Jack McCoy often fall into the heroic lawyer category. Television hero lawyers are very popular. In fact, a 1993 poll revealed that two of the twelve most-admired attorneys were fiction characters from television, *Matlock* and *Perry Mason*.[5] Perry Mason certainly always possesses what Rosenbaum describes as a presidential timbre. Jack McCoy always presents a noble persona, accepting nothing less than the letter of the law. And Ben Matlock, though extremely cheap, consistently saves the innocent defendant from a justice system that cannot seem to properly investigate a crime or care to know the truth. Note that we write of these lawyers in the present tense. These courtroom dramas and legal procedurals are still played on television as well as most of the movies. This means that their messages are still being cultivated.

To be sure, the fictional hero lawyer follows the ABA's *Model Rules of Professional Conduct*.[6] The most important rule is that a lawyer must provide competent representation (rule 1.1). Lawyers must be knowledgeable of the law and be thorough and prepared. Our most noble television lawyers will make every effort to become familiar with the case and always know the law. They will use what little resources they have in order to investigate the crime their clients are accused of. They will engage in self-sacrificing and zealous representation (rule 1.3), never encourage a client to engage in illegal behavior (rule 1.2(d)), make a false statement of fact or law (rule 3.3(a)(1)), or encourage perjury (rule 3.3(a)(3)). There are eight major categories of rules in the ABA's *Model Rules of Professional Conduct*. The television/movie lawyer violates these rules when in desperation, disillusioned, vengeful, or obtuse.

The disillusioned lawyer is frequently found in the movies and on television. It is not uncommon for the hero lawyer to go through a point of disillusionment. Often, hero lawyers find themselves in situations where the law does not seem to work in favor of the innocent, and they struggle through their disillusionment before they are able to save the day. Movies such as *The Lincoln Lawyer*, *Michael Clayton*, and *The Firm* feature lawyers who learn that sometimes it takes committing a crime in order to obtain justice or to see that justice must be preserved.

Obtuse attorneys play the courtroom game, looking for shortcuts, and lose their morals and the truth in justice along the way. Lieutenant Daniel Kaffee (played by Tom Cruise) in *A Few Good Men* starts as an obtuse lawyer never going to trial and viewing his dealings as successes, but he redeems himself becoming a hero of justice by uncovering the true criminal.

Obtuse lawyers are often criminal. In the popular television series *Suits*, the lawyers are concerned with money, power, and most of all winning—by any means necessary. Attorney Annalise Keating in *How to Get Away with Murder* has no qualms about breaking the law to win a case. And Dr. Jason Bull, from CBS's legal procedural, uses a team of experts to pry into the lives of the jury in order to win trials. Dr. Bull and his team are presented as heroes, yet they violate many laws, including invasion of privacy and jury tampering.

Thus far, most of the above discussion has focused on the defense attorney. As mentioned earlier, movies tend to focus on defense attorneys. Legal procedurals are more likely to give prosecutors more air time. In *Law & Order*, the prosecutors dominate the second half of the show. In the *Law & Order* spin-offs, prosecutors play a small role but are portrayed in a positive light. *Major Crimes*, though a police procedural, includes a prosecutor who has a powerful role in each episode guiding the detectives on the legality of their investigations. *Law & Order* was discontinued in 2010 after twenty years of high ratings. However, in 2017, we were introduced with a new, much stronger focus of the prosecutor with *Chicago Justice* (see Box 7.1). In *People vs. O.J. Simpson: American Crime Story* both the prosecution and the defense attorneys are covered in detail. True crime docudramas, such as *The Prosecutors*, give the most weight to prosecutors today, focusing on their pursuit of justice within the system.

Box 7.1.   *Chicago Justice*: The New *Law & Order*

In March of 2017, Dick Wolf, the creator of *Law & Order*, launched a new legal procedural which gave almost exclusive focus to the prosecution. Where prosecutors dominated the second half of *Law & Order*, *Chicago Justice* is a true legal procedural that dedicates more of the show to the prosecution and the courtroom with some inclusion of detectives investigating crimes. If the show survives, it could mean a revitalization of the centrality of prosecutors over defense attorneys in the courtroom. What is interesting about this show is that the prosecutors recognize the influence the media has on their job but do the best they can to fight crime and ensure that justice is served. They believe in the law and work well with the police, but sometimes the law is not enough and change must be advocated.

Chicago Justice does with prosecutors what so many courtroom dramas do with defense attorneys. It shows that prosecutors do not blindly follow the law in a war on crime. Instead, prosecutors are depicted to be conscious, informed members of society enforcing the law but also working to improve it. They are true protectors of the people. The show is not without its stereotypes. As with most crime and justice television programs and movies, the main justice official is a white male. Women and minorities are not ignored, however. While the star of the show is Assistant State Attorney (ASA) Peter Stone, a white man, his boss is State Attorney Mark Jefferies, a black man. ASA Stone is often partnered with female ASA Anna Valdez. Additionally, Puerto Rican Detective Antonio Dawson is partnered with Detective Laura Nagel. Although it appears that the show has covered all of the major races, even including an Asian actor, it still depicts white males as the primary defenders of justice. We will see how the show develops with time.

Lawyers and Performing Bodies

Jason Bainbridge argues that even if the lawyer is not the central character in a legal procedural, the *performing* bodies still send an important message.[7] The message is that court appearances are performance pieces that require lawyers to engage the "audience" (i.e., the judge and jury). Thus, lawyers do not uncover truth, instead they create narratives of the truth and the best narrative wins. Bainbridge makes a case for this performance. It is the lawyer's physicality and rhetoric that "persuades and ultimately constructs 'the truth' in each case."[8] In his analysis of the internationally popular program *Ally McBeal*, Bainbridge claims that legal procedurals have erased gender, regardless of the fact that she is always shown wearing mini skirts and concerned about personal relationships. However, the very fact that she is one of the few very popular television lawyers is telling of gender, as we see in so many of the media constructs. If the performing body is important to our understanding of truth and justice, then the presentation of fictional lawyers tells us that the white male is the personification of truth and justice. We examine some of the messages that these performing bodies tell us in Box 7.2.

Box 7.2.   *How to Get Away with Murder*: Race, Gender, and Greed

In *How to Get Away with Murder*, race and gender are simultaneously very heavy issues and not issues at all. Though defense attorney Annalise Keating is constantly pushed down for being black and a woman, she is still presented as a strong character who is capable of having her own strengths and weaknesses. She is not created to be simply the "strong black woman." Though she is indeed a strong woman, the creators of the show do not make her untouchable or unlovable like so many black women in the media. She is still capable of creating strong bonds with her students and lovers alike.

Annalise is also a law professor who mentors her students by selecting the best to work on her private practice cases. Through this work, her students learn how to apply the law and gather evidence. Among her law students, race and gender are portrayed very eloquently. The females are not shown in a different or lesser light than the male students and are shown as just as capable and intelligent. Though race is indeed presented as an issue, it is shown in regards to overcoming racism and discrimination. The students, regardless of race and gender, continue to flourish through all their adversity. The students are never shown as racists, with the exception of one student. Asher Millstone is an ignorant, white, heterosexual male and displays sexist and homophobic views. However, the group tends to beat this out of him at every turn.

The show is not without its stereotypes, however. For example, every black character has a "rags to riches" storyline. Wes is the lost puppy whose mother committed suicide at a young age and has been on his own for many years, steadily treading his way up the societal totem pole. Annalise was born into a poor black family with a mother who continues to belittle her at all turns, regardless of her accomplishments. And Michaela was a foster child adopted by a white family who was extremely racist against her. Michaela cuts her family ties and proceeds to "make something" of herself. And Connor is the promiscuous gay male who like so many male characters shuns emotional intimacy.

Justice is never truly obtained in the show in regards to Annalise and her students, though they do win a few of their own cases. Annalise is the stereotype of the criminal defense attorney who will do and say anything to win a case. She also encourages a culture of unethical behavior among her students, perpetuating the stereotype of the crooked attorney.

Throughout the show, they all break laws from extortion to murder in order to win cases as well as cover up a murder, hence the title.

The police seem very competent throughout the show but are constantly stumped and stymied by Annalise, her students, and Nate (the black police officer in cahoots with Annalise), Annalise, and her students. The same could be said for the prosecutors and judges depicted throughout the show's course. They are very competent but face a wall of corrupt cops and lawyers and students all trying to stop officials from uncovering the truth.

If you knew nothing of defense attorneys, the court system, and law school, this is not the show to watch if you wish to feel confident in our justice system. Each episode contains at least one corrupt official and many verdicts are not reached or are reached with falsified evidence. Many murders go unsolved and most in the show are committed by our law students, lawyers, and police officers.

INFOTAINMENT AND TELEVISED TRIALS

Televising Famous Trials

Although Americans have been captivated with cameras in the courtroom since the 1935 Lindbergh baby kidnapping/murder, it was not until 1991, when Courtroom Television Network (Court TV), gave the public a true taste of the infotainment factor in the courtroom. In 1991, Court TV was launched with a case about a twenty-three-year-old murder and a case of a Cincinnati rape by a former college basketball star.[9] Court TV provided live coverage of famous cases like the Menendez brothers' murder in 1993 and the O. J. Simpson case in 1995. These cases drew in millions of viewers and helped to rejuvenate the public's love of a good court case.

Angelique Paul wrote that while Court TV was "voyeurism, pure and simple,"[10] it still worked to educate the public about how the court really worked. However, Alicia Kinlay points out that court trials are not simply televised allowing the audience to engage in passive viewing.[11] Instead, the network selects cases that are newsworthy and bring the most profit. This misrepresents the types of crime, the amount of crime, the context of crime, and the victim–offender relationship, thus reinforcing the same first-order and second-order cultivation that other forms of media create. Robert Ferguson wrote of televised trials, "its control of the angle of vision is absolute."[12] The television cameras show the people in certain angles that bring out the appearance of emotion, even when none exists. Furthermore, when people are able to see the trial first hand, they are more likely to accept the verdict.

Court TV was not the only or the first network to broadcast a criminal case. One of the first fully televised trials was the 1961 Jerusalem trial of Nazi war criminal Adolf Eichmann, drawing millions of viewers worldwide.[13] Within the United States, one of the first televised trials to draw in a large viewing was *People v. Steinberg*.[14] In this case, Joel B. Steinberg was a lawyer who brutally beat to death his adopted daughter. The case brought on a debate of whether or not cameras should be allowed in the courtroom. In this case, the judge, the defense attorney to some extent, and the jury welcomed the cameras, while the prosecution and the defendant were not as welcoming. Among supporters, it was believed that cameras are beneficial or neutral, definitely exciting, and potentially improve the defendant's (i.e., Steinberg's) image. However, Steinberg believed that the cameras kept him from having a fair trial.

Televised trials have captivated the American public. Such trials include the 1979 trial of serial killer Ted Bundy, the 1995 O. J. Simpson murder trial on Court TV (see Box 1.1), the 1993 Menendez murder trials on Court TV, the 1991 William Kennedy Smith rape trial on CNN, and so many more. Court TV aired most of the famous cases, while CNN aired others. TMZ. com also joined the fray with the Lindsay Lohan verdict in 2010. As Court TV evolved, it was relaunched as TruTV in 2008, eliminating coverage of criminal trials. Headline News (HLN), initially launched as CNN2 in 1982, covers the occasional criminal trial, such as the 2011 trial of Casey Anthony charged with murdering her two-year-old daughter, as well as the 2011 trial of Dr. Conrad Murray for the death of Michael Jackson.

Reality Court Television

While Court TV, CNN, HLN, and other such news networks bring cameras into the courtroom and provide an entertainment factor, other networks have created entertainment courts. The first of such shows was *The People's Court* with Judge Wapner which aired from 1981 to 1993. The program was a half-hour court that relied on binding arbitration. *The People's Court* was not a true legal court of law. Judge Wapner heard each party's case and no lawyers were allowed. Parties were required to follow his ruling. Following Judge Wapner's retirement, *The People's Court* has hired other "judges," including Ed Koch (1997–1999), Jerry Sheindlin (1999–2001), and Marilyn Milian (2001–present). Other popular reality television court shows include *Judge Hatchett*, *Judge Joe Brown*, *Judge Judy*, *Judge Mathis*, and *Hot Bench*. Other than Judge Wapner's tenure, reality television judges tend to perform for the camera in a very authoritarian and rude manner similar to shows like *The Real Housewives* and their spin-offs.

Weblink 7.1

For a detailed listing and description of reality court television programs, go to Judge Shows: Court in Session! at: http://judgeshows.com.

Real Court and Broadcasting

All is not lost, however, since we can also find live broadcasting of real court proceedings. Many courts, including appellate and supreme courts, allow cameras in the courtroom, though with some limitations. The U.S. Supreme Court is reported to be the least accountable branch in government. Furthermore, it has been increasingly partisan. This has led to very unpopular decisions in the eyes of both Republicans and Democrats.[15] In 2007, Senator Arlen Spector introduced a bill that would permit televising Supreme Court proceedings. The bill's purpose was to enable transparency and accountability of the highest court in the country. Opponents to this bill believed that cameras in the courtroom would result in grandstanding slightly similar to reality court television, compromise the anonymity and security of the court, and provide the court's activities out of context. This bill did not pass and the Court still does not allow cameras in its courtroom. However, audio recordings of U.S. Supreme Court hearings can be obtained. C-SPAN posts various oral arguments heard by the U.S. Supreme Court. In this way, the court enables a level of transparency. At the state level, all fifty states allow

Figure 7.1. Illinois Supreme Court Justice Robert R. Thomas (left), Illinois Supreme Court Chief Justice Rita B. Garman (center), and Justice Mary Jane Theis (right) hear the appellate case of *In re Estate of Sheldon*, 2017. Photo in the public domain.

Figure 7.2.   Attorney Darrell K. Seiglar in oral argument to the Illinois Supreme Court in the case of *In re Estate of Sheldon*, 2017. Photo obtained from the Illinois Supreme Court Oral Argument Audio & Video-2017 website and with permission of Mr. Seigler.

cameras in their courtroom.[16] The Illinois Supreme Court, for example, has allowed cameras since 1983 and even posts daily videos.[17] We can also find televised court cases in the lower state courts on Courtroom View Network.[18] While we still see that most lawyers do, in fact, tend to be white and male, we also see the true nature of the profession. We can see the intelligence, commitment, and decency of most lawyers in action.

Weblink 7.2

To listen to U.S. Supreme Court oral arguments, go to C-SPAN at: https://www.c-span.org/search/?sdate=&edate=&searchtype=Videos&sort=Most+Recent+Event&text=0&sponsorid%5B%5D=1133&formatid%5B%5D=33.

CONCLUSION

Lawyers, judges, and the courts have not been a strong focus of the media in the past decade. However, we know that of the three subfields of criminal justice, the court with all of its workings is the most respected and trusted. The public take for granted that the court holds to the highest standard of justice. This does not mean that the public does not hold negative beliefs about this field. We know that the media is where most people obtain their "knowledge" of crime and justice. We also know that the media cultivate beliefs about crime and justice. While lawyers and judges are not portrayed as fighting a violent war on crime, their constant inclusion in crime movies, television programs, and news stories tell us that they are part of that war. On the one hand, the media tell us that prosecutors have the best interests of the people at heart, as they work zealously to convict criminals. On the other hand, the media also tell us that without defense attorneys most incarcerated people would be innocent. We receive messages on both sides. However, since the media are flooded with police fighting a war on crime, we are pushed further to commit to a conservative ideology of law and order.

Chapter 8

Prison in the Media

MEDIA VERSUS REALITY

Among the three subfields of criminal justice, we know the least amount about corrections. Where the court is the least accountable institution in criminal justice, corrections institutions are invisible. Through the media, we see a war on crime fought by the police and continued by prosecutors. We see offenders convicted of crimes and get sent to prison. But that is where most of our knowledge stops. When the media cover corrections, they typically show us life in prison. Most of our media exposure of corrections comes from prison movies, docudramas, and documentaries. Movies such as *Cool Hand Luke*, *The Longest Yard* (1974, 2005), *Escape from Alcatraz*, *The Shawshank Redemption*, and *The Green Mile* show us the corruption and inhumane conditions of prisons. However, these movies do not give us the bigger picture.

Data released by the Bureau of Justice Statistics tell us that, in 2015, there were just over 1.4 million state and federal prison inmates.[1] While most television programs and movies focus on males, females represent 111,495 state and federal prison inmates. The racial makeup of the U.S. prison population was 34 percent white, 35 percent black, and 22 percent Hispanic. Prisons are long-term incarceration facilities that secure more-serious offenders, that is, those convicted of felonies. Jails, on the other hand, secure less-serious offenders, typically for up to one year.

In 2014, there were 744,600 jail inmates in the United States. Where women represented about 7 percent of the prison population, they represented 15 percent of the jail population.[2] The racial makeup of the U.S. jail population was 47 percent white, 35 percent black, and 15 percent Hispanic. We see that black men are overrepresented in prisons. Prison is where the media place most of their focus. However, there were 4.6 million adults on probation in 2015.[3]

About 75 percent of probationers were male. Slightly over half (55 percent) were white, 30 percent were black, and 13 percent were Hispanic.

Regardless of the number of people sentenced to probation, the media only address this type of sentence in passing. Most people do not even know the difference between probation and parole.[4] Likewise, the media typically address prisons, not jails. Most people do not know the difference between a prison and a jail. And herein lies the problem. Far more people obtain their "knowledge" of corrections, and specifically prisons, from the media, than they do of crime, police, and the courts.

Examining news coverage of criminal justice, Steven Chermak found that the news covered the police in 52 percent of the crime stories. The courts were covered in 30 percent of the crime stories, and corrections were covered in 4 percent of the crime stories.[5] If you consider crime news stories in which correctional institutions were mentioned in some manner, the coverage increased to 17 percent. In this chapter, we examine prisons in the media. However, even though prisons are not widely covered, any coverage in the media is all of the information most people receive. The invisibility of prisons increases the probability that the media will cultivate perceptions. Let us examine what is cultivated.

FRAMING AND NARRATING PRISONS IN MOVIES

One of the earliest known prison movies is a short silent prison comedy titled *Convict 13* and starred the famous Buster Keaton. In the film, while Keaton is unconscious, an escaped inmate switches clothes with him. Following the narrative of that time, Keaton is mistaken for the escaped inmate and is hauled off to prison to be hung. While the short film does not waste time disparaging the prison officials, the fact that his identity is not identified and they are willing to hang an innocent man displays a narrative that prison officials are similar to the Keystone Kops. Keaton is able to escape the noose but is confronted by a very large and very violent inmate. This, and a prison riot that covers his identity, points to the terrible conditions of prisons. Many of the prison films of the 1920s were slapstick comedy. *Condemned!* is probably the first serious prison movie. The film doubles for a love story as inmate Michel falls in love with the warden's wife. While Michel was guilty of the crimes that put him in prison, he is unjustly punished when the warden learns of the love affair. The movie portrays corrupt officials and extremely harsh prison conditions. Michel is able to escape the prison, but like so many movies of the time the bad guy is always caught.

Media researchers have uncovered four main narratives in prison movies starting at the time of talking movies.[6] A dominant narrative within prison movies was the nature of confinement (1929–1942). This narrative, like most crime movies of the time, criticized the harshness of society. Prison movies during this era typically presented the inmate as innocent. He was wrongfully convicted, framed, or was forced into crime by the horrible social circumstances plaguing society. In this narrative, corrections officers were highly oppressive, even criminal, though the warden tends to be a decent person. The circumstance of the innocent inmate being kept by the criminal corrections officers has been referred to as corrections backwards law. In these movies, the inmates were heroes. If we examine prisons in the media, we find that the focus is usually on the inmate. *The Big House* is consistently identified as one of the best prison movies. In this movie, John Morgan is imprisoned for a one-time check forgery. He is a decent individual being kept in a violent, overcrowded prison by corrupt officials but a good warden. Morgan undergoes a metamorphosis and ends up a hero by helping to minimize injuries during a prison riot.

The second prison movie narrative is the pursuit of justice (1943–1962). In this narrative, inmates are not portrayed as innocent. They take responsibility for their crimes. These movies no longer condemn the prison and its officials. Instead, they focus on hardened criminals and the hard life in prison. Although inmates are living in harsh and violent conditions, they are redeemable. Still, escape is not uncommon. There are many prison movies that use this narrative, including famous movies like *Men without Souls*, *The Birdman of Alcatraz*, and *Convicts 4*. *Men of San Quentin* focuses on a warden telling a story of widespread corrections backwards law. In this movie, Holden fights his way to the position of warden and institutes prison reform. He is ultimately successful in reforming the harsh conditions of the prison and of the hardened prisoners themselves.

The third narrative dominated between 1963 and 1980 and is referred to as the authority and control correctional film. In this narrative, inmates are not as violent as they are portrayed in the previous era, the negative view of the correctional system is reintroduced, and there is a theme of universal corruption. Corrupt corrections officers are referred to as "smug hacks" and inmates are heroes. The prisons are very isolated, which allows for total exploitation of the inmates. It is during this era that rape, racism, and drugs are introduced as prison problems. *Cool Hand Luke* is usually identified as one of the best prison movies. In this movie, Luke (played by Paul Newman) is incarcerated and put on the chain gang for breaking parking meters when he was drunk. Luke is defiant of the corrupt system and refuses to bow down to their expectations. He is beaten and put in the isolation box repeatedly. *Brubaker* uncovers a case of extreme corruption and mass murder in an Arkansas prison. *Attica*, *The Longest Yard* (1974 and 2005), and *Escape from Alcatraz* are also placed in this narrative.

The last prison movie narrative has been identified as freedom and release (1981–present). In this narrative, prisons take on a more science fiction, futuristic nature. They are portrayed as colonies or prisoner transport systems. Violence in these prisons is extreme and corruption is rampant. Inmates are heroes and guards are crazy. In *Escape from New York*, the crime rate is so high that the entire island of Manhattan is made into a prison with no guards. Ex-Special Forces and armed robber Snake Plissken is sent in to rescue the president within twenty-two hours or have an implanted explosive blow off his head. Of course, the hero inmate saves the day. Other well-known movies that use this narrative are *Escape Plan*, *Get the Gringo*, and *Lockout*. You can also find prison scenes with this narrative in *Guardians of the Galaxy* and *Chronicles of Riddick*.

While these narratives have been found to prevail during the aforementioned eras, there are many movies in which the narratives can be found out of time or to overlap. For example, *The Shawshank Redemption* clearly follows the freedom and release narrative but also follows the authority and control narrative. *The Green Mile* follows the nature of confinement.

Weblink 8.1

Explore hundreds of Prison Movies released in several countries since the 1920s at: http://www.prisonmovies.net/.

Stock Characters and Stock Plots in Prison Movies

Nicole Rafter provides a detailed analysis of typical, or stock, prison movie characters and plots.[7] In prison movies, the cast has three major characters: the convicts, the warden, and the corrections officers. In early movies, there were typically three main convicts: the main inmate who is a hero, the hardened criminal, and the snitch. Often the hero convict had a convict buddy who may serve as a hero in his own right. Three famous movies exemplify these characters. In *The Big House*, Morgan is the hero, Butch is the hardened criminal, and Kent is the snitch. We see these three characters throughout prison movie history. In *The Shawshank Redemption*, Andy is the hero inmate, Red is the convict buddy, Tommy Williams is the snitch, and Bods Diamond and the Sisters is the prison rape gang. In *The Longest Yard*, Paul Crewe is the hero inmate. Caretaker, who also plays hero as he smuggles highly coveted goods into the prison, is the convict buddy. Skitchy Rivers is the snitch, and Turley is the psychotic inmate.

The next major character is the warden. Depending on the era, the warden is paternalistic or cruel. In the first narrative, nature of confinement, the warden is typically portrayed as decent. These wardens can be found in *The Big House, Brubaker,* and *Men of San Quentin.* Most prison movies, however, portray wardens as indifferent or very corrupt. Under the warden, corrections officers tend to be very violent. In most prison movies, even the movies discussed earlier, the main corrections officer characters tend to be violent and exploitative.

Throughout the four narratives, main plots tend to revolve around escape and survival. Nature of confinement narratives tend to feature escape because the inmate is wrongly convicted. These movies include *The Shawshank Redemption, Chronicles of Riddick,* and *Escape Plan.* In other prison escape movies, the harsh conditions of prison life push the inmate, guilty or not, to attempt escape. These movies include *Escape from Alcatraz, Escape from New York, Escape Plan,* and *The Rock.* Prison riots tend not to be the main event but tend to find their way into most prison movies. However, *Riot* and *Attica* have the riot as their central theme.

Survival is another plot found in most prison movies as the conditions are portrayed as very harsh. In *The Shawshank Redemption,* before Andy plots his escape, his every move is an attempt to survive the inmate violence and the administrative corruption. The plot of *The Longest Yard* is winning the football game against the corrupt prison guards in order to regain a level of self-respect. Likewise, *Cool Hand Luke* tries to survive an oppressive prison system.

Prison Rape

Prison rape is a common "stock theme" in today's prison movies. Prison movies either include rape scenes or make reference to the rape of an inmate. The frequency of rape in movies cultivates a belief that most inmates either experience rape as a victim or an offender. Yet, victimization reports identify that only 12 percent of male inmates are raped, a figure too high for sure.[8] Helen Eigenberg and Agnes Baro examine the images of male rape in a sample of prison movies and found that 60 percent include attempted or completed rape. Some of these movies are *American History X, Escape from Alcatraz, Sleepers,* and *The Shawshank Redemption.* Furthermore, most movies that did not include rape were character studies of a particular person such as *Birdman of Alcatraz, Cool Hand Luke, Murder in the First, The Green Mile,* and *The Hurricane.* In other movies, the hypermasculine character is able to fight off attempts of rape, such as in *Escape from Alcatraz.*

An additional factor of prison rape is race. Of the movies examined by Eigenberg and Baro, rape was either intra-racial (white-on-white) or unclear.

However, in society, it is typically assumed that rapists are minorities. (See our discussion of the symbolic assailant in Chapter 3.) In prison movies, the rapist is usually another inmate, though research shows that staff and corrections officers also frequently rape inmates. The prison rape is also depicted as very violent or involving a weapon. The victim is typically young, medium-built, and is depicted as effeminate or gay. Additionally, in most prison movies, the rapist is severely punished, typically with extreme violence. However, most prison rape complaints go unsubstantiated. They conclude that much of the rape inclusion is used for sensational value.[9] These depictions follow all of the social constructs of prison sexual assault, with the exception of race. And while most prison movies are about male prisons, most prison rapes occur against female juvenile secure residents (i.e., young female inmates).

RACE AND PRISON

We opened this chapter with some statistics on race. According to the Bureau of Justice Statistics, black inmates represent 35 percent of the state and federal prison population. This fact stands in light of the fact that black people represent 13 percent of the U.S. population and 27 percent of all arrests. They represent a large portion of the prison population but a small fraction of prison inmates in the movies. Further, it is rare that a black actor is cast as the lead inmate in a prison movie bringing us back to Weaver's argument that producers do not want their programs to be viewed as "minority programs."[10] *The Green Mile* is the only prison movie discussed here (we include the most famous) in which the star inmate is black. And yet, we still find strong beliefs that black men are the violent predators and rapists of our society. In discussing the representation of prison rape, Andrew Sargent tells us about a New York criminal court judge who, in 1981, would not sentence a young, middle class, white male to Rikers Island (the city jail) because he would most certainly be raped by a black or Hispanic inmate, "We take judicial notice of the defendant's slight build, his mannerisms, dress, color, and ethnic background and are cognizant of the unfortunate realities that he would not last for ten minutes at Rikers Island. . . . the State of New York could not guarantee his safety in prison surroundings. . . . [He] would be immediately subject to homosexual rape and sodomy and the brutalities from fellow prisoners such as make the imagination recoil in horror (brackets added)".[11]

While we seldom see minority inmates starring in prison movies, we are more likely to see them featured in prison documentaries or docudramas.

PRISON ON TELEVISION

Prison Television Series

The topic of corrections and prisons is thin in televisions dramas. Like news coverage, corrections is the least covered area of criminal justice. And similar to news reports, inclusion of corrections in crime dramas tends to be an incidental inclusion in any given episode. During a criminal investigation, it is common for a detective to visit an inmate in prison in order to obtain desperately needed information. In crime dramas, it is not uncommon for a criminal to have flashbacks of prison life. However, it is not very common for television to dedicate an entire series to prison. The earliest well know prison show is *Hogan's Heroes*. Similar to the first prison movies of the 1920s, this show was a comedy. The show was about prisoners of war being held captives by Nazi's. The inmates were the ones in control, aside from being able to escape, and the Nazi's were portrayed as Keystone Kops. However, while the show had a lot of humor, it diminished the seriousness of Nazi torture and the conditions of prisons in general. This show was given six years to send the message that prisons are not that bad.

Similar to prison movies, television prison dramas are hard to find. A Google search reveals the same nine shows in the United States: *Hogan's Heroes*, *Women in Prison*, *Oz*, *Prison Break*, *The Prisoner*, *Breakout Kings*, *Alcatraz*, *Orange Is the New Black*, and *Prison Break: Sequel* (mini-series, 2017). We could not find prison shows prior to the 1950s, and most shows did not last long, often running for one or two seasons. Today, when most people think about prison shows, the shows that come to mind are *Oz*, *Prison Break*, and *Orange Is the New Black*.

Similar to prison movies, the focus is on the inmate and the violent, overcrowded, and corrupt conditions of prisons. Prison is portrayed as extremely violent, and violence is often met with cheers and encouragement. In *Oz*, even popular characters are killed. The very dangerous inmate and the snitch inmate found in prison movies also exist in television shows. Prison rape is very common but unlike prison movies, consensual same-sex sex and relationships are also common. Additionally, following the stereotype, gay men are very promiscuous. Also similar to prison movies, the stars are predominantly white males.

Prison Docudramas

Moving a bit closer to the realities of prison, we must move to the docudramas. However, recall that docudramas are a form of infotainment. They are incomplete and tend to be edited in order to draw in audiences. Just like docudramas of courtrooms, the camera angles, the lighting, and the music reveal a situation that may not be real. We also see people grandstanding in front of the camera. The more common prison/jail docudramas include *60 Days In*, *Behind Bars*, *Inside American Jail*, *Jail*, *Lockup*, *Locked Up Abroad*, and *Women in Prison*.

Most of these docudramas feature female inmates as well as minorities. With most of the television dramas and the docudrama, most inmates are portrayed as repeat offenders and the prison or the jail (commonly featured in docudramas) is viewed as a stepping stone, making secure facilities ineffective. In corrections research, this has been identified as turnstile justice or revolving-door justice. Ray Surette argues that the continued recycling of movie themes since the 1920s provides a media loop of prison ineffectiveness.[12] This increases the belief that turnstile justice is much more common than it really is. However, we must also consider that while many of the prison movies and television shows purport to uncover the terrible and dehumanizing conditions of prisons, in the end they mostly serve as entertainment.

Prison Documentaries

The most accurate media portrayals of prisons and prison life can be found in documentaries. Yvonne Jewkes reminds us that prison documentaries are similar to ethnographic research of ethical dilemmas or inhumane circumstances.[13] Documentaries may show the hard life within overcrowded prisons and jails. For example, *Behind Bars* reveals the terrible prison conditions in San Quinten Prison, while *MegaJail* shows the overcrowding, violence, and long pretrial detentions of the Miami jail. Other documentaries focus on violence and riots in prisons, such as *Behind Bars: Riot in New Mexico*. The death penalty has been a controversial sentence since the 1970s, and documentaries such as *Into the Abyss* try to bring some light to the humanity of the death row inmate. *One for Ten* examines wrongful convictions in death penalty cases. This documentary claims that one in ten death row inmates is wrongfully convicted.

Some documentaries reveal the conditions of youth in corrections. *Lock Em Up! Juvenile Injustice at Rikers Island Prison*, covering the cruel treatment of children, was just one more source of information that preceded the 2017 announcement of the closing of Rikers Island jail. *Tattooed Tears* revealed the harsh conditions juveniles were placed in as the California Youth Authority treated the 11,000 young offenders under their care like hardened adult criminals. Today, the system of juvenile corrections has been overhauled. Now called the California Division of Juvenile Justice, it only confines 1,200 youth.

Another special population focused on in documentaries is women. Though women represent a much smaller portion of the inmate population, they represent over 8 percent (over 100,000) of the prison population. However, the prisons tend to be ill-prepared for the special needs of women inmates, such as prenatal care, childcare, gynecological care, and menopausal care, to name a few. Documentaries such as *Mothers of Bedford* show the inadequacy of prisons that house more pregnant women than they can accommodate. Yvonne Jewkes warns us that although documentaries appear to be ethnographic studies of prisons, there is still manipulation of the facts.[14] She describes that director Michael Apted (*21 Up*) admitted to camera and image manipulation when he believed that one individual would soon end up in prison. Jewkes also argues that like prison movies, most documentaries do not influence prison reform. We can speculate that documentaries may simply reinforce preexisting ideologies.

Figure 8.1. Alcatraz prison sign. Photo courtesy of iStock.

Weblink 8.2

Visit Prison Photography for a description of "The 23 Best American Prison Documentaries" at: https://prisonphotography.org/2013/11/17/the-20-best-american-prison-documentaries/.

WOMEN IN PRISONS

Criminology research has consistently found that female offenders are typically punished for stepping out of gender role expectations. We see this with harsher sentencing when women engage in very serious crime that society typically thinks of as male crime. Media research finds similar presentations of female offenders. Typical media portrayals of female offenders include images of criminal women as unattractive, bad wives, bad mothers, insane, manipulative, young (i.e., infantalization), and sexually deviant; otherwise, their crimes are self-defense.[15]

The movie *Chicago*, though it may seem to some like an ode to femininity and how powerful a woman can be, is actually extremely sexist. Everything that happens to the women in the prison and everything that they end up with is because of the men in their lives and the sexualization of the female body. Each woman in the movie has been imprisoned for the same wrongdoing, though their ways of carrying out the deed are different, murdering her male intimate partner. This might not seem like a big deal to a casual viewer. However, on closer examination, one realizes that when every woman revolves around a man, her own value is pushed to the background. Men, despite the fact that there are few in the movie, once again become the main focus. Even Velma and Roxie, though they eventually make their way out of prison and into the real world, are able to do so because of the male gaze. Their seemingly sole purpose in life, besides being freed from prison, is to make it big by flaunting their sexuality.

The women residing in the prison, though dressed modestly in their prison garb, are changed to varying degrees by seductive costumes for each musical number. They are not allowed to sing even the "Cell Block Tango," which explains why they have all been imprisoned, without being forced to change into slinky outfits made simply for sex appeal. Even in a world without men (the prison), these women are depicted as seductresses and sexual beings— their entire identities still striving for male appreciation. Not only are the women in this movie sexualized to a high degree, but there is also a sort of infantalization of Roxie when she is presented to the public and the court. She is made to dress demure and keep her look soft and shy. She is also portrayed as a clueless victim, even going so far as to depict her as a puppet on her male lawyer's strings in one of the musical numbers. She is supposed to be young and pure and pretty for the courts and the media so as to make them trust her. Referring to Chapter 7, we see that not only did the lawyer perform for the audience but he also knew the power of performance. *Chicago* is more likely to be categorized as a legal movie, but it skirts both the courts and corrections. And while our discussion centers on sex and sexism, women in prison movies also include other narratives that men in prison movies do (see Box 8.1).

Box 8.1.   Race, Gender, and Corruption in *Orange Is the New Black*

In *Orange Is the New Black* though the prison is shown as a distinctly lackluster building lacking in color, it is also depicted as somewhat homey through the bonds and families that the characters make. However, this home is not without its prison problems or stereotypes. Race, rape, drugs, and corruption are major problems that run through the series. Most of the guards in this show are white males who abuse their authority simply to feel powerful. They are extremely sexist and racist. The one white male guard who was neither sexist nor racist did not last long in the show after impregnating a Hispanic female inmate in a scandalous affair. In the beginning of the show one of the guards (nicknamed Porn Stache by the inmates) proceeds to rape multiple inmates and use the drug-addicted inmates to traffic drugs throughout the prison. When one woman is killed, he covers his tracks by making it look like a suicide.

The female offenders in this show keep themselves segregated by race. Though only a few of the women seem blatantly racist, many make underhandedly ignorant racist comments throughout the show. Much of the inmate racism seems to stem from ignorance and naivety rather than true hatred of other races. The main character, Piper, is a white woman put in jail for drug trafficking but she never comes across as racist throughout the show. She seems to be able to insert herself into any racial demographic shown (though not particularly well in some cases), and though she is indeed the main character, her importance and centrality seem to fade as the show progresses. The race of Piper is significant, however, as once again the star is a non black individual. While black women in the U.S. prison population are incarcerated at more than twice the rate of white women, once again a white inmate is central. Although this prison show features more black inmates than most, the casting of a white actress avoids the "Black program" label. However, the critique of white middle-class privilege appears to give the show an explanation for the casting.

Anne Schwan argues that *Orange Is the New Black* serves as a covert call for prison reform and "has the potential to mobilize social awareness and activist sensibilities."[16] Jewkes would argue that this would be a bold claim.[17] If you knew nothing about prisons and female offenders, this would be the show to watch. First, it is the only currently running women in prison series on television. Second, it shows much of the gritty realities of the prison systems and how they are structured to fail the women they incarcerate. Finally, while we do not conclude that the show will enable prison reform, we do promise that you will be entertained.

PRISONS IN THE NEWS

As mentioned earlier, corrections is a focus in less than 5 percent of the crime news stories. News tends to focus on negative stories. Stories often focus on the failure of prisons to protect the public, and prison escapes are common corrections stories in the news. For example, in 2015, the news followed a story in which a female prison tailor fell in love with an inmate and helped him and another inmate escape. Both had been serving time for murder.[18]

In an experiment, researchers found that the framing of prison escapes works to increase anxiety and fear.[19] Specifically, when the news report followed a standard format, which frames prison breaks as something to fear, then anxiety and fear of crime are increased for older people. Failure to protect the public also includes failing to protect inmates from each other and from prison staff. Recently, a large amount of news coverage was given to the inhumane conditions of Rikers Island in New York City.[20] News stories also focus on lack of punishment and inmate coddling as well as what Surette identifies as correctional horrors.[21] The individual stories of Rikers Island was followed with the announcement that the facility will be closed. A review of corrections news stories reveals that similar to prison movies and television programs, inmates tend to be the focus in more of the stories.

Bill Yousman examines discussions of prison on primetime television. He finds that news coverage often covers crime and issues around corrections in a racist manner. Beginning in the 1960s, the war on crime was found to be a war on urban crime committed by black males to be feared by white America.[22] In 1988, William "Willie" Horton was a black inmate who was charged with assault, armed robbery, and rape while on weekend furlough (i.e., release from prison for a brief period of time as a result of good behavior). Willie was already serving a prison sentence for murder. Willie's case was covered in the news in countless stories and became the face for the war on crime in the 1988 Bush/Dukakis Presidential campaign. One advertiser admitted that he purposely chose a photo that would be "every suburban mother's greatest fear."[23] Remember, crime was code for black.

CONCLUSION

The topic of prisons is not very popular in the media. Though we are still in an era of mass incarceration, prison movies and television programs do not reflect this. And though these programs, as well as news stories, are far and few in between, they still manage to cultivate certain beliefs about criminal offenders and prisons. David Wilson and Sean O'Sullivan report that in the 1930s, sixty prison movies were released.[24] Until the 1980s, about 500 prison movies were released, resulting in about ten movies per year. This is a drop in the bucket compared to the number of movies released each year. The same portion can be found for television crime series, docudramas, documentaries, and news stories. Overall, prison themes are not popular and do not do well. However, because the narratives, stock plots, stock characters, and crime and justice ideologies tend to be reproduced time and again, prison in the media tends to reaffirm the need for incarceration. As Wilson and O'Sullivan claim, prison movies are subtle propaganda for our conservative ideologies.

Chapter 9

Conclusion

Media's Social Construction of Crime and Justice

Most members of society, fortunately, do not have direct exposure to crime and justice. As a result, they rely on the media for their crime and justice "knowledge." The social constructions put forth by the media tell us who is likely to commit crime, which crimes are more likely to occur in society, and how often they occur. They tell us about race, gender, income, age, and religion. Social constructs also tell us how the justice system fights crime and how effective they are. While the media did not single-handedly create these social constructs out of thin air, as they are constructs already found in society, they have helped to reinforce various political agendas. These constructs guide our ideologies on how crime should be dealt with.

In the first part of this book, we examined the different forms of media separately, describing how each form constructs crime and justice. However, as you read through each chapter, you saw common themes and ways of creating these themes. We found common narratives of crime, criminals, police, lawyers, courts, and prisons. Within each frame of storytelling, the media presented liberal ideologies as well as conservative ideologies. We also learned that though the story of crime and justice is told through the various media forms, the messages we receive are consistent over time and over medium. This consistency allows for first-order cultivation, guiding general perceptions. These are the frames for crime and justice. The consistency in crime and justice storytelling also creates second-order cultivation, guiding our attitudes and evaluations about crime and justice that result from frequent media exposure. These are the narratives we become familiar with. Social construction and cultivation are ultimately the power of the media.

CRIME IN THE MEDIA

The media love a good crime story. We can see this through the fact that, with the exception of weather and traffic, the media dedicate more time to crime than other topics, including sports. Although crime reporting has decreased in the past seven years, it still represents a large portion of news reporting.[1] Furthermore, news commentary represents between 46 percent and 85 percent of reporting on national news channels. This provides ample opportunity to impart messages of crime.

First, the media tell us that crime is a major problem in our society. The time allocated to crime reporting alone tells us that it is more common than we understand it to be. However, the time dedicated to televisions shows, fictional and reality, and the types of movies released reinforce what the news tell us. If we examine Nielson ratings, we see that crime dramas rank pretty high on a weekly basis. Box office statistics also tell us the crime movies do very well. In fact, most blockbusters are of the crime genre, even when the subgenre is comic or science fiction. Second, the media tell us that crime is violent and serious. It is rare to see a news story, television show, or movie about nonviolent crime. Additionally, murder, rape, and terrorism are by far the most common crimes addressed in the media.

The third piece of information that the media provide is that crime is an urban problem. In the 1980s, as discussed in Chapter 8, this became a presidential platform with Willie Horton as the poster boy for crime.[2] The reporting, as well as the majority of television and movie crime programs that already focused on urban crime, reinforced this notion. Fourth, crime is presented as a black male, or at least a non white, activity. News stories still reinforce the symbolic assailant and superpredator belief which entails a young black male who is very violent and cannot be stopped unless arrested and incarcerated. Even when research finds that whites are more likely to be the focus of criminals, black males are more likely to be shown in custody, thus, presenting the dangerous nature of black men. And though television shows and movies are not nearly as likely to hire non white actors, the racial distribution is more likely to show minority actors as criminals and white actors as justice officials, most being male.

Although all media programs and reporting do not represent these images all of the time, their frequency reinforces and sometimes creates first- and second-order cultivation that crime is a serious, frequent, violent, urban, minority, male problem in our society. The television programs that focus on white wealthy criminals tend to be portrayed as out of the ordinary, even if we see them frequently. This reinforces perceived reality of crime as an urban minority problem. As most people obtain their "knowledge" of crime from the media and as criminal justice policy is strongly influenced by public perceptions and demands, the media have a powerful influence on crime control policy. With the U.S. culture still in a conservative era, this results in tough-on-crime demands resulting in more police, more arrests, and mass incarceration. This also helps to justify society's practice and support of racial profiling.

POLICE IN THE MEDIA

No one is better qualified to lead the United States' war on crime than the police. Media images tell us that the police are noble, tough, men who are highly trained to fight crime. We do not deny that the vast majority of police are well intentioned in their continuous efforts to keep the public safe. Furthermore, most police departments enjoy the ability to recruit former military personnel. However, the presentation of the police as highly trained is vastly overstated by the media.

Most police departments are located in rural areas with small budgets and rarely are crime labs available at their fingertips. Most police officers in the nation do not possess a college degree or have worldly experiences to understand cultural diversity. The average police training academy in the nation runs four to six months. The average police department does not require any lengthy law education; they certainly do not require law school education. Most police officers do not have scientific training either. All of this results in limited pre-job training and a lot of on-the-job training. We also know that police are members of the same society that gets its crime and justice "knowledge" from the same media as everyone else. They are also susceptible to the pressures of the politicians and the public who cry for immediate and tough action.

Simultaneously, the police are portrayed as ineffective by the media. News reports dedicate more attention to police misdeeds than to their successes. The successes tend to be represented as arrests made and criminals and escaped prisoners apprehended. But rarely are the police activities that bring the communities together shared in the media, at least not in major headlines. Stories of school resource officers/teachers, police citizen academies, and police outreach and storefronts must be directly searched for in the news to be known. When an offender is arrested or the police are in an investigation, we often see the police chief surrounded by commanding officers giving press releases updating the public on their efforts. On the one hand, these are positive images showing us that the police are working hard to fight the war. On the other hand, these images are often used to show that the police are fighting a losing battle. As a result, we need other non police crime fighters to keep us safe.

The media, in telling us that the police need help, present this as a team effort or they can present this as a Keystone Kop situation. In most police procedurals, police are often aided by CSIs or amateur detectives. They also work with prosecutors in order to ensure the case will stand up in court. In most of these cases, the police are aided because they do not have the expertise or the resources. However, many of the programs show the police as incompetent and sometimes uncaring. In many cases, the detective is the star and the police are inconsequential to solving the case or they are completely absent. Then we have the victims who must solve their own cases rather than the corrupt police who are more criminal than crime fighter. However, most news stories, reality television, and docudramas still use the police as the gatekeepers of information. This tells us that they are the most reliable source of information. They are to be trusted.

With the presentation of crime as a major problem of violence in our society and with the mostly high trust and confidence in the police, we depend on them to fight the war on crime. We welcome the artillery the police bring with them to mass shootings, such as Columbine and Sandy Hook. We also welcome highly armed police who investigate terrorists. It then becomes normal for highly armed police to "keep the peace" during protests and less violent criminal investigations—this with the continued media image of police.

COURTS IN THE MEDIA

The lawyers and the courts are not well addressed in the media. However, we still have a positive image of them, mostly. Prosecutors are seen as officers of the court. And they are. But they are also, and foremost, law enforcement. As such, prosecutors are our friends—if we are law abiding, of course. Prosecutors work with the police to investigate crimes and bring criminals to justice. And the judge gives them the harsh sentences the public demands. The defense attorney does not have as good a reputation in society as does the prosecutor. When news reports give attention to defense attorneys, they are often giving press releases about their clients. In most cases, these clients are being tried and convicted in the public court of law that is led by the media. However, most courtroom dramas and legal procedurals have at their center the defense attorney.

Courtroom dramas and legal procedurals both on television and in the movies tend to be told through the eyes of the defense attorney. It is here that we learn that while the justice system always "gets its man," it also often gets the wrong man. It is up to the defense attorneys to investigate the crime to uncover the true criminal, which enables the innocent client to go free. We learn that the police and prosecutor are not as effective as we are led to believe. And unless the defense attorney also "fights crime," the justice system will trample on the innocent citizens of society. However, we are not left without images of the criminal or unethical defense attorney that we see in so many television shows. So our law-and-order ideologies are left intact.

CORRECTIONS IN THE MEDIA

Corrections is the least addressed field of criminal justice in the media. It is unpopular, does not receive high ratings, and is not as profitable as police and crime programs. However, we do know that we need the corrections system. In particular, we need the jails and prisons. We have already learned that crime is a major urban problem of violence perpetrated by minority males. We have already learned that police are working hard in a war on crime and that the prosecutors and judges help them to keep us safe. However, we are not truly safe unless there is a place to lock up these hardened criminals. And never mind if that place is horribly violent as we have been told by the media throughout the history of our modern prison system. We need prisons! Since the media lead us to believe that crime is so frequent and violent, which fortunately is not always the case, we cannot fathom a society that is reluctant to incarcerate its criminals.

Prisons are the institutions the media tell us criminals must go. After all, prisons are so violent because criminals are violent. We see the police working so hard fighting the war against crime, and we must remove these dangerous felons from society. However, we can find a few inmates who do not belong in prison. These inmates are capable of developing lifelong friendships and saving the people around them, emotionally and bodily. And, yet, no one is safe in prisons or jails, as we learn from the media. The media tell us of a corrections backwards law in which not only are the inmates criminal but so are the guards. And while we consistently cry for prison reform in this country, prison is the first place we turn to in our war on crime; otherwise, we would not have widely used terms like mass incarceration.

The media tell us that prisons are ineffective. Concepts like turnstile justice, revolving-door justice, and imprisonment binge tell us that offenders go in, come out, and go back in. Why? Because prisons do not work! Dr. Garcia once knew a detective who called prisons and juvenile secure facilities training grounds. Officials see a lot of repeat offending. But then officials see the worst of society. Media also focus on the repeat offenders in their news stories and in their crime/inmate characters. We are led to wonder that if everyone is a repeat offender and how and when their life of crime started? Regardless of the ineffectiveness of prisons, we are told that letting these offenders walk free is the worst thing we can do. Now we are not advocates of opening up the prison doors and letting everyone out never to be incarcerated again. However, we also know that most inmates have drug abuse or mental health problems. We also know that the research shows that drug rehabilitation and psychological/psychiatric counseling is much more effective than incarceration.[3]

RACE, GENDER, CRIME, AND JUSTICE

Throughout this book, we have dedicated a section to race and gender within each chapter. However, if you read more closely, you will see that race and gender are intertwined with all of our topics. As we have described earlier, criminals are symbolically equated with maleness and minority status, while justice is equated with maleness and whiteness. This is not a radical statement. This is not a call to arms or a feminist cry, though we are proud feminists! This is an observation that has been recognized by researchers for decades, as well as by most journalists. Without the assumption of the symbolic assailant, we would not have racial profiling, a practice recognized by the government for quite some time. We would also not have more whites represented in arrests but more blacks represented in prisons. And the media work to reinforce these stereotypes, prejudices, and discrimination. As a result, the media are part of the system of oppression.

Gender is another status that the media inadvertently oppress. Though women are not depicted as more criminal than they are in reality, they are depicted as a certain type of person. We have previously written that minor crimes do not sell in the media. Well, females as a group commit less serious crimes than do males. Males represent, by far, the larger portion of offenders in all crime types, except for embezzlement and prostitution/commercial vice. This tells us that as a group, females are less frequent and less serious offenders. This also tells us that females engage in "women's work" in crime. But this does not sell news stories, movie tickets, or television ratings.

When the media focus on women, as with all other crimes, they tend to focus on the worst crimes but also the crimes that are not deemed to be gender-related. The serious killer or the drug dealer are fodder for media profits. However, since this is not women's work, women are portrayed as unfeminine, evil, and bad women (bad mothers and sexually deviant lesbians). These images are not media images alone, these are society's stigmas for women who step out of their prescribed gender roles. And just like racial and ethnic minorities, women are not portrayed as capable of fighting crime. This is told by their very absence in these roles or by their supporting roles.

LESSONS LEARNED

In 1956, Horace Miner published the "Body Ritual among the Nacirema."[4] The story told of an anthropologist who learned of a culture who was obsessed with the body as ugly. The culture, though possessing a highly developed economy, relies on ritual and magic to right the body it despises. In order to fix the problems of the body, people worship privately in front of shrines within their homes on a daily basis. The more powerful a family the more shrines within one's home. Within the Nacirema, children are taught how to worship at these shrines from a very early age. Of importance to the shrine is the charm box where members gather various charms and magic potions provided by medicine men who write in an ancient language. As the ritual goes, every day members of the family enter the shrine, bow before the charm box, and mingle holy water from a font in a rite of ablution. The body ritual continues from there and becomes more entailed and more bizarre. Miner also describes other rituals of the Nacirema involving other members of this society who are believed to possess magic, such as holy-mouth men and witch doctors.

The story is one of Garcia's favorites and she likes to use it in her classes. The lesson is that we cannot know a people and the details of their culture unless we truly study that culture. Until that time that we uncover the realities of that culture we make all sorts of outlandish assumptions that to members of the culture are quite normal and perceived quite differently. In this case, we use the media to understand that culture. The media here represent the doctor. And the culture represents the American culture, it is Nacirema spelled backwards. So the shrine with its charm box and holy waters represent the bathroom with its sink and medicine cabinet. The medicine men, holy-mouth men, and witch doctors are the doctors, dentists, and psychologists within our society. Garcia loves this story and encourages you to read it!

Weblink 9.1

Read Miner's story of the Nacirema at the Michigan State University at: https://msu.edu/~jdowell/miner.html.

The lesson here is that you cannot know until you know. With so many students telling Garcia that they want to work in law enforcement because they want to see action and with so many African American students stating that racial profiling is necessary because black people commit most of the crime (YES, Garcia hears this all of the time!), we can see the power of the media. With public cries for more police, more arrests, and more imprisonment, we can see the power of the media. Again, the media do not create these ideologies. However, since most people receive their "knowledge" of crime and justice from the media, there is an indirect positive relationship between the media and crime and justice policy.

We must become a more informed society. Garcia likes to provide her students with a video of a State Farm commercial in which a woman is dating a man who claims to be a French model. If you have seen this commercial, you immediately know that he is not a French model, but she believes it because she learned about it on the internet. Garcia uses this as example to inform her students that you cannot take everything that you receive from the media at face value. You must explore the issues. If you do not have a school library available to you, then you can use the public library. Google Scholar and Google Books are great search engines once you learn how to sift out the government and advocacy documents and get at the research. Once you explore the reality of crime and justice you will be a more informed consumer and more productive member of society. This book is not a call to drop your conservative law-and-order ideologies or liberal due process ideologies. Instead, it is a call to investigate the truths of crime and justice. It is a call to view media with a critical eye, and to take television programs and movies for what they truly are, entertainment.

Appendix A

Crime Movies Cited with Release Dates

Air Force One (1997)
American History X (1998)
American Hustle (2013)
American Snipper (2014)
Anatomy of a Murder (1959)
Attica (1980)
Aurora Teagarden (2015–)
Bad Boys II (2003)
Bad Lieutenant (1992)
Beverly Hills Cops (1984–1994)
The Big House (1930)
Birdman of Alcatraz (1962)
The Birth of a Nation (1915 and 2016)
Black Magic (1949)
Bonnie and Clyde (1967)
The Bourne Identity (2002–2016)
The Brave One (2007)
Brubaker (1980)
Bruce Almighty (2003)
Catch Me If You Can (2014)
Charlie's Angels (2000)
Charlie's Angels: Full Throttle (2003)
Chicago (2002)
CHIPS (2017)
Chronicles of Riddick (2004)
Concrete Evidence (2017–)
Condemned! (1929)
Convict 13 (1921)

Convicts 4 (1962)
Cool Hand Luke (1967)
Cop Land (1997)
CopyCat (1995)
Crash (2004)
Dark Blue (2002)
The Dark Knight (2008)
DC 9/11: A Time of Crisis (2003)
Death Wish (1974–1994)
The Departed (2006)
Die Hard (1988–2007)
Dirty Harry (1971–1988)
End of Watch (2012)
The Equalizer (2014)
Escape from Alcatraz (1979)
Escape from New York (1981)
Escape Plan (2013)
Evan Almighty (2007)
Falling Down (1993)
Fargo (1996)
The Fast and the Furious (2001–2017)
A Few Days in September (2006)
A Few Good Men (1992)
The Firm (1993)
Flight 93 (2006)
Flower Shop Mystery (2016–)
Four Brothers (2005)

Free State of Jones (2016)
Furious 7 (2015)
Gangs of New York (2002)
Gangster Squad (2013)
Garage Sale Mystery (2015–)
Get the Gringo (2012)
The Godfather (1972–1990)
Godfellas (1990)
Gone Girl (2014)
Gran Torino (2008)
The Green Mile (1999)
Guardians of the Galaxy (2014)
Hailey Dean (2016–)
The Hamburg Cell (2004)
Heaven Can Wait (1978)
Heist (2001)
Hot Shots (1991 and 1993)
The Hurricane (1999)
Inception (2010)
Inherit the Wind (1960)
Jack Ryan: Shadow Recruit (2014)
Judgement at Nuremburg (1961)
Kill Bill (2003–2004)
L.A. Confidential (1997)
Lakeview Terrace (2008)
Leon: The Professional (1994)
Lethal Weapon (1987–1998)
The Lincoln Lawyer (2011)
Lockout (2012)
London Has Fallen (2016)
Lone Survivor (2013)
The Longest Yard (1974 and 2005)
Man on Fire (2004)
The Matrix (1999)
Menace II Society (1993)
Men of San Quentin (1942)
Men without Souls (1940)
Michael Clayton (2007)
Miss Congeniality (2000)
Mission Impossible (1996–2015)
Mississippi Burning (1988)
Monster (2003)
Mr. & Mrs. Smith (2005)
Mulholland Falls (1996)

Murder in the First (1995)
Murder She Baked (2015–)
My Cousin Vinny (1992)
Naked Gun (1988–1994)
Natural Born Killers (1994)
New York (2009)
No Rest for the Wicked (2011)
Ocean's Eleven (2001)
Oh, God! (1978)
Olympus Has Fallen (2013)
Payback (1999)
Philadelphia (1993)
Police Academy (1985–1994)
Public Enemies (2009)
Pulp Fiction (1994)
RED (2010)
Reign over Me (2007)
Riot (1969)
Robocop (1987 and 2014)
The Rock (1996)
Salt (2010)
Selma (2014)
September 11 (2002)
Serpico (1973)
Set It off (1996)
The Shawshank Redemption (1994)
Sherlock Holmes (2009 and 2011)
Silence of the Lambs (1991)
Sleepers (1996)
Spy (2015)
Straight Outta Compton (2015)
Sum of All Fears (2002)
Super Trooper (2001)
S.W.A.T. (2003)
Taken 2 (2012)
Takers (2010)
The Thief Catcher (1914)
A Time to Kill (1996)
The Town (2010)
The Transporter (2002–2015)
To Kill a Mockingbird (1962)
Tower Heist (2011)
Training Day (2001)
True Lies (1994)

12 Angry Men (1957)
21 Jump Street (2012)
22 Jump Street (2014)
Twin Towers (2003)
United 93 (2006)
The Untouchables (1987)

Veronica Mars (2014)
White House Down (2013)
The Wizard of Oz (1939)
World Trade Center (2006)
WTC View (2005)
Zero Dark Thirty (2012)

Appendix B

Television Shows Cited with Air Dates

Alcatraz (2012)
Alias (2001–2006)
Ally McBeal (1997–2002)
American Detective (1991–1993)
The Americans (2013–)
America's Most Wanted (1988–2012)
The Andy Griffith Show (1960–1968)
Angie Tribeca (2016–)
Animal Kingdom (2016–)
APB (2016–)
Barney Miller (1974–1982)
Behind Bars (1994–1995 and 2011)
Behind Bars (2008)
Behind Bars: Riot in New Mexico (2001)
Better Call Saul (2015–)
Blue Bloods (2010–)
Boardwalk Empire (2010–2014)
Bones (2005–2017)
Boston Legal (2004–2008)
Breaking Bad (2008–2013)
Breakout Kings (2011–2012)
Brooklyn Nine-Nine (2013–)
Bull (2016–)
Cagney & Lacey (1981–1988)
Car 54, Where Are You? (1961–1963)
Castle (2009–2016)
Chicago Justice (2017–)
CHiPs (1977–1983)

City Confidential (1998–2006)
The Closer (2005–2012)
Cold Case (2003–2010)
Cold Case Files (1999–)
Cold Case Files (2017–)
Conviction (2016–2017)
Cops (1989–)
Covert Affairs (2010–2014)
Criminal Minds (2005–)
CSI: Crime Scene Investigation (2000–2015)
CSI: Cyber (2015–2016)
CSI: Miami (2002–2012)
CSI: NY (2004–2013)
Dateline (1992–)
Dexter (2006–2013)
Dick Tracy (1937 and 1945)
Dragnet (1951–1959; 1967–1970; 2003–2004)
The Dukes of Hazzard (1979–1985)
Elementary (2012–)
FBI: The Untold Story (1991–1993)
The First 48 (2004–)
Forensic Files (1996–)
Franklin & Bash (2011–2014)
Gangland (2007–2010)
Good Behavior (2016–)
Gotham (2014–)
Hawaii Five-O (1968–1980; 2010)

Hill Street Blues (1981–1987)
Hogan's Heroes (1965–1971)
Homeland (2011–)
Hot Bench (2014–)
How to Get Away with Murder (2014–)
Inside American Jail (2007–)
JAG (1995–2005)
Jail (2007–)
Judge Hatchett (2000–)
Judge Joe Brown (1997–)
Judge Judy (1996–)
Judge Mathis (1998–)
Justified (2010–2015)
Kojak (1973–1978)
L.A. Law (1986–1994)
Law & Order (1990–2010)
Lie to Me (2009–2011)
Locked Up Abroad (2007–)
Lock Em Up! Juvenile Injustice at Rikers Island Prison (2011)
Lockup (2005–2017)
Low Winter Sun (2013)
Major Crimes (2012–)
Marvel's Agent Carter (2015–2016)
Matlock (1986–1995)
MegaJail (2011)
The Mentalist (2008–2015)
Monk (2002–2009)
Mothers of Bedford (2011)
Mr. Robot (2015–)
Murder She Wrote (1984–1996)
NCIS (2003–)
NCIS: Los Angeles (2009–)
NCIS: New Orleans (2014–)
Numbers (2005–2010)
Orange Is the New Black (2013–)
Oz (1997–2003)

PBS NewsHour (1975–)
Perception (2012–2015)
The People's Court (1981–)
People vs. O.J. Simpson: American Crime Story (2016–)
Perry Mason (1957–1966)
Person of Interest (2011–2016)
Police Story (1973–1979)
Police Woman (1974–1978)
Prison Break (2005–2009)
Prison Break: Sequel (mini-series, 2017–)
The Prisoner (2009)
The Prosecutors (2000–)
Psych (2006–2014)
Quantico (2015–)
The Real Housewives (2006–)
Rizzoli & Isles (2010–2016)
Sherlock (2010–)
The Shield (2002–2008)
60 Days In (2016–)
Sleepy Hollow (2013–)
Snapped (2004–)
Sons of Anarchy (2008–2014)
Southland (2009–2013)
Starsky & Hutch (1975–1979)
Suits (2011–)
Tattooed Tears (1979)
Top Cops (1990–1994)
True Crime with Aphrodite Jones (2010–)
24 (2001–2010)
21 Up (1977)
Veronica Mars (2004–2007)
White Collar (2009–2014)
The Wire (2002–2008)
Women in Prison (1987–1988)

Notes

CHAPTER 1

1 Plea bargaining refers to the process by which the defendant pleads guilty to the charge or a lesser charge in exchange for a lighter sentence. This is done to save the government the astronomical costs of going to trial or of potentially losing the case.

2 *Merriam-Webster*, available at http://www.merriam-webster.com/dictionary/medium.

3 Dahl, "Trayvon Martin Shooting."

4 Schwartz, "10 Best Hip Hop Protest Songs since the Trayvon Martin Shooting."

5 Fasching-Varner, Reynolds, Albert, and Martin, *Trayvon Martin, Race, and American Justice.*

6 Turow, *Media Today*, 13.

7 Grossberg, Wartella, and Whitney, *MediaMaking*, 271.

8 Grossberg, Wartella, and Whitney, *MediaMaking*, 273.

9 Robinson, *Media Coverage of Crime and Criminal Justice*, 12.

10 At the time this book was being written, CBS and Viacom discussed a merger that failed to go through.

11 Robinson, *Media Coverage of Crime and Criminal Justice*, 20.

12 Garcia, "Constructing the 'Other' within Police Culture," 68.

13 Trask, "The Shocking Moment a Homeless Man Attacks a Woman with a Wooden Stake on a Busy Street in Melbourne."

14 Throughout this book we will omit the release dates of movies and television programs within the chapters, unless vital to our discussion. Refer to Appendix A for a full listing of all movies discussed with their release dates and Appendix B for a full listing of television programs and their airing dates, including documentaries which are typically released to television.

15 *Law & Order*, "Volunteers."

16 Martinez, "South Carolina Cop Shoots Unarmed Man."

17 Keating, *Hollywood Lighting from the Silent Era to Film Noir.*

18 Gerstenfeld, *Hate Crimes*, 133.

19 Surette, *Media, Crime and Criminal Justice*, 5.

20 Hixson, *Murder, Culture, and Injustice*, 203–204.

21 *The Tonight Show with Jay Leno*, "The Dancing Ito's."

22 *CBS News*, "O.J. Simpson Trial."

23 Lichtblau, *Bush's Law*.

24 *Survivor* refers to family members of murder victims or people who survive a crime.

25 FBI, *"Uniform Crime Reporting,"* last modified 2017, https://ucr.fbi.gov/.

26 FBI, *Crime in the United States, Table 1*.

27 FBI, *2015 Crime Clock Statistics*.

28 McLaughlin, "Murders, Shootings and Gun Sales per Day."

29 Harrell, *Workplace Violence against Government Employees, 1994–2011*, 7.

30 Amy, "Judiciary School," 130.

31 Neubauer and Fradella, *America's Courts and the Criminal Justice System*, 176–77.

32 "Innocence Project" (2016).

33 Cullen and Jonson, *Correctional Theory*, 2.

34 Hu, "6 Ex-Rikers Guards Sentenced to Prison in Attack on Inmate."

35 Probation is a community sentence given in lieu of jail or prison. Whereas, parole is a community sentence inmates serve when released from jail or prison but are still under supervision. In each case, there are conditions that probationers and parolees must fulfill. For example, they are required regular visits with the supervising officer, they cannot reoffend, they cannot use drugs, they cannot abuse alcohol, they cannot associate with felons, and they must hold a job or go to school if they are juveniles. Other conditions are applied on a case-by-case basis.

36 Kaeble, Maruschak, and Bonczar, *Probation and Parole in the United States, 2014*, 1.

37 Cullen and Jonson, *Correctional Theory*, 39.

38 Zgoba, Witt, Dalessandro, and Veysey, *Megan's Law*, 37–39.

39 Garcia, "Constructing and Reconstructing Female Sexual Assault Victims in the Media," 34; Surette, *Media, Crime and Criminal Justice*, 189.

CHAPTER 2

1 Rafter, *Shots in the Mirror*, 77.

2 Welch, Fenwick, and Roberts, "State Managers, Intellectuals, and the Media," 223.

3 Muraskin and Domash, *Crime and the Media*, 2.

4 Surette, "Some Unpopular Thoughts about Popular Culture," xvi.

5 Surette, *Media, Crime and Criminal Justice*, 16.

6 *New-York Daily Times,* "Conviction for Arson," 2.

7 Websdale and Alvarez, "Forensic Journalism as Patriarchal Ideology," 126–28.

8 Authors were not typically listed in early newspapers.

9 Office of the Historian, "U.S. Diplomacy and Yellow Journalism, 1895–98."

10 Surette, *Media, Crime and Criminal Justice*, 17.

11 Surette, *Media, Crime and Criminal Justice*, 16.

12 Pooley, "Grins, Gore, and Videotape," 37.

13 Hamilton, *Channeling Violence*, 276.

14 CNN, "CNN's First Broadcast: June 1, 1980."

15 Gilboa, "The CNN Effect," 29.

16 Grossberg, Wartella, and Whitney, *MediaMaking*, 15–26.

17 Gottfried and Shearer, *News Use across Social Media Platforms 2016*, 1.

18 Roughly 67 percent of the U.S. adults use Facebook.

19 Anderson and Caumont, "How Social Media Is Reshaping News," 4.

20 Rakes, "Indiana Woman Arrested after Father Records Video of Alleged Child Abuse, Posts it on Facebook," 1.

21 Crime Sider Staff, "Driver Arrested for Texas Motorcycle Crash Caught on Video," 1–2.

22 Fenton, "Suspects in Wyman Park Stabbing Filmed the Assault, Posted to Facebook," 1–3.

23 CBS Detroit, "2 Accused of Beating Up Disabled Man, Posting Video on Facebook," 1–2.

24 Gingras, Moghe, and Grinberg, "Quick-Thinking McDonald's Worker Leads Police to Facebook Killer," 5.

25 Today, "Share Your Visit."

26 CNN, "Complete Coverage on Social Media."

27 "TheRightists.com," 1.

28 Mahashari, "How Fake News Goes Viral."

29 Lubbers, "There is No Such Thing as the Denver Guardian, Despite That Facebook Post You Saw," 2.

30 Kang, "Fake News Onslaught Targets Pizzeria as Nest of Child-Trafficking."

31 Balmas, "When Fake News Becomes Real," 446.

32 Schwartz, *Broadcast Hysteria*, 3–11.

33 See chapter 3, for a discussion of the symbolic assailant.

34 Morin, "Framing Terror," 987.

35 Washington Post Staff, "Donald Trump Announces a Presidential Bid."

36 Foreman, Artega, and Collins, "The Role of Media Framing in Crime Reports," 8.

37 Gerstenfeld, *Hate Crimes*, 101–2.

38 Foreman, Artega, and Collins, "The Role of Media Framing in Crime Reports," 9.

39 Mallicoat and Ireland, *Women and Crime*, 193.

40 Mallicoat and Ireland, *Women and Crime*, 36.

41 Fox59, "3 Suspects Charged in Rape, Abduction at Castleton Hotel."

42 Mallicoat and Ireland, *Women and Crime*, 228.

43 FBI, *Crime in the United States, 2015*, Table 33.

44 Belknap, *The Invisible Woman*, 115.

45 Mallicoat and Ireland, *Women and Crime*, 228.

46 Garcia, "Aileen Wuornos," 642.

47 Garcia and Butler, "White Collar Crime Enforcement."

48 Stabile, "Getting What She Deserved," 318.

49 See Murphy, "The Intractability of Reputation," 217.

50 Stabile, "Getting What She Deserved," 317.

CHAPTER 3

1 Surette, *Media, Crime and Criminal Justice*, 37.

2 Morin, "Framing Terror," 1.

3 Surette, *Media, Crime and Criminal Justice*, 41.

4 Lysiak, "Why Adam Lanza Did It," 3.

5 Sasson, *Crime Talk*, 13.

6 Sasson, *Crime Talk*, 38–51.

7 Grinberg and Sholchet, "Brock Turner Released from Jail after Serving 3 Months for Sexual Assault," 2.

8 Nordheimer, "Youth, 14, Draws 9 Years to Life in Killing of 4-Year-Old."

9 McNamara, "Lionel Tate Gets 30 Years in Jail," 4.

10 Ashford, "The Queens Precinct Where Stop-and-Frisk Survives," 17.

11 Lacey-Bordeaux, "Police Rescue Autistic Boy's Birthday Party," 5.

12 Death Penalty Information Center, *The Death Penalty in 2016*, 3–6.

13 Rafter and Brown, *Criminology Goes to the Movies*, 88–91.

14 Rafter and Brown, *Criminology Goes to the Movies*, 94–96.

15 Sweeney, Schmadeke, and Meisner, "How to Stop Guns, Gangs and Poverty?" 7.

16 Marsh, "Revenge Porn Victim to Google," 6.

17 Bult, "Former Doctor Convicted of Four Revenge Killings in Omaha," 1.

18 Thielking, "Gun Violence Spreads Like an Infectious Disease," 3.

19 Mallicoat and Ireland, *Women and Crime*, 352.

20 Garcia, "Constructing and Reconstructing Female Sexual Assault Victims in the Media," 32–33.

21 Garcia, "Constructing and Reconstructing Female Sexual Assault Victims in the Media," 18–37.

22 Grinberg and Sholchet, "Brock Turner Released from Jail after Serving 3 Months for Sexual Assault," 1.

23 Grinberg and Sholchet, "Brock Turner Released from Jail after Serving 3 Months for Sexual Assault," 23.

24 Blay, "Black Voices," 3.

25 Blay, "Black Voices," 7.

26 King, "Brock Turner, Corey Batey Show How Race Affects Sentencing," 1.

27 Bandura, Ross and Ross, "Imitation of Film-Mediated Aggressive Models," 4.

28 Bandura, "Social Cognitive Theory of Mass Communication," 266.

29 Kaplan, "Why Violent Video Games Are Good for Kids," 2.

30 Alforte, "Video Games Effects on Child Development," 3.

31 Murphy, "Pennsylvania Man Kills Toddler in WWE Wrestling Imitation," 1–2.

32 History.com Staff, "Columbine High School Shootings," 1.

33 Kimble, "Memories of a Massacre," 2–3.

34 Bergen, "The Golden Age of Terrorism," 4.

35 Note that while the white supremacist hate group the Ku Klux Klan has engaged in extreme terroristic acts, they have not been commonly known as a terrorist group.

36 Morin, "Framing Terror," 989.

37 Bengali and Linthicum, "San Bernardino Shooter was a Pakistani Who Became Known as a 'Saudi Girl,'" 4–6.

38 Prokupecz and Conlon, "NYPD: Hatchet Attack an Act of Terror," 6.

39 Ali and Abdullah, "Did the Patriot Act Change US Attitudes on Surveillance?" 13.

CHAPTER 4

1 Statista, "Global Box Office Revenue from 2016 to 2020."

2 Hamilton, *Channeling Violence*, 276.

3 Grossberg, Wartella, and Whitney, *MediaMaking*, 3–32.

4 Surette, *Media, Crime and Criminal Justice*, 37.

5 Garcia, "Constructing and Reconstructing Female Sexual Assault Victims in the Media," 34.

6 Morin, "Framing Terror," 4.

7 Surette, *Media, Crime and Criminal Justice*, 41.

8 *Wisconsin v. Mitchell*, 508 U.S. 476 (1993).

9 Morin, "Framing Terror," 2.

10 Rafter, *Shots in the Mirror*, 189; Ray, *A Certain Tendency of the Hollywood Cinema, 1930–1980*, 59.

11 Ray, *A Certain Tendency of the Hollywood Cinema, 1930–1980*, 59.

12 Ray, *A Certain Tendency of the Hollywood Cinema, 1930–1980*, 59.

13 Rafter, *Shots in the Mirror*, 198.

14 Sasson, *Crime Talk*, 89.

15 Rafter and Brown, *Criminology Goes to the Movies*, 7.

16 Tonry, *Punish Race*, 38.

17 Rafter, *Shots in the Mirror*, 112.

18 Grossberg, Wartella, and Whitney, *MediaMaking*, 20.

CHAPTER 5

1 Release dates of television program can be found in Appendix B.

2 Nielson, "Top Ten."

3 Nielson, "Tops of 2016: TV."

4 Maeder and Corbett, "Beyond Frequency," 103.

5 Jockel and Fruh, "'World Ain't All Sunshine,'" 197.

6 Turnbull, "Crime as Entertainment," 824.

7 Reactive policing refers to responding to crimes, as opposed to working to prevent crime from happening in the first place.

8 Stevens, *Media and Criminal Justice*, 13.

9 Maeder and Corbett, "Beyond Frequency," 84.

10 Maeder and Corbett, "Beyond Frequency," 87.

11 Maeder and Corbett, "Beyond Frequency," 88.

12 Maeder and Corbett, "Beyond Frequency," 89–92.

13 Weaver, "The Role of Actors' Race in White Audiences' Selective Exposure to Movies," 370.

14 Jockel and Fruh, "'World Ain't All Sunshine,'" 200.

15 Morton, Tillman, and Gaines, "Serial Murder," 4.

16 Cavender and Fishman, "Television Reality Crime Programs," 12.

17 Valenzuela and Brandao, "Historical Dramas, Current Political Choices," 450.

18 Cavender and Fishman, "Television Reality Crime Programs," 7.

19 Oliver and Armstrong, "The Color of Crime," 21.

20 Garcia, "Snapped," 10.

21 Berrington and Honkatukia, "An Evil Monster and a Poor Thing," 59.

22 Berrington and Honkatukia, "An Evil Monster and a Poor Thing," 69.

23 Hapke, *Girls Who Went Wrong*, 1.

24 Helfield, "Poisonous Plots," 161.

25 Bureau of Labor Statistics, *American Time Use Survey Summary*, 15–16.

CHAPTER 6

1 Cullen and Jonson, *Correctional Theory*, 108.

2 Surette, *Media, Crime and Criminal Justice*, 86–87.

3 Miller, "The Motion Picture Production Code of 1930," 2225.

4 Boyd, "Drug Films, Justice, and Nationhood," 270–271.

5 Surette, *Media, Crime and Criminal Justice*, 88–89.

6 Surette, *Media, Crime and Criminal Justice*, 90.

7 Johnson, "Special Message to the Congress on Crime and Law Enforcement."

8 Johnson, "Special Message to the Congress on Crime and Law Enforcement."

9 Joseph, "Soldiers of Baltimore," 3.

10 Campbell and Campbell, "Soldiers as Police Officers/Police Officers as Soldiers," 328–29.

11 Campbell and Campbell, "Soldiers as Police Officers/Police Officers as Soldiers," 329.

12 CBS News, "Ferguson State of Emergency Ends after Days of Protests," 5.

13 Reaves, *Hiring and Retention of State and Local Law Enforcement Officers, 2008 Statistical Tables*, 12–13.

14 Durose and Burch, *Publicly Funded Forensic Crime Laboratories*, 1.

15 Innocence Project, "Exonerate the Innocent," 1.

16 Vester, "Bodies to Die for," 31.

17 Harris, "Charlaine Harris."

18 Garcia, "Difference in the Police Department," 333.

19 Langton, *Women in Law Enforcement, 1987–2008*, 1.

20 IMDB, "Top-US-Grossing Crime Titles."

21 Garcia, "Assessing the Current Status of Women in Policing," 171.

22 Garcia, "'Difference' in the Police Department," 340.

23 Ray, *A Certain Tendency of the Hollywood Cinema, 1930–1980*, 59.

24 Weaver, "The Role of Actors' Race in White Audiences' Selective Exposure to Movies," 370.

25 Barlow and Barlow, *Police in a Multicultural Society*, 1.

26 Garcia and Cao, "Race and Satisfaction with the Police in a Small City," 195.

27 Garcia and Cao, "Race and Satisfaction with the Police in a Small City," 197.

28 Ross, "A Multi-Level Bayesian Analysis of Racial Bias in Police Shootings at the County-Level in the United States, 2011–2014," 12–13.

29 Tate, Jenkins, and Rich, "Fatal Force."

30 Graziano, Schuck, and Martin, "Police Misconduct, Media Coverage, and Public Perceptions of Racial Profiling," 54.

31 Seewer, "How Police Departments with Consent Decrees Are Faring."

32 Ellison, "Growing Political Influence of Police Unions Derails Consent Decrees," 3.

CHAPTER 7

1 Brust, "The 25 Greatest Legal Movies," 2.

2 AMC Filmsite, "Greatest Courtroom Dramas."

3 Pollack, "Whatever Happened to Atticus Finch?" 133.

4 Rosenbaum, "The 6 Types of Lawyer Movies," 47–50.

5 Paul, "Turning on the Camera on Court TV," 656.

6 ABA, "Model Rules of Professional Conduct."

7 Bainbridge, "The Bodies of Law," 396.

8 Bainbridge, "The Bodies of Law," 409.

9 Sventkey, "Introducing Court TV," 4.

10 Paul, "Turning on the Camera on Court TV," 694.

11 Kinlay, "Televised Court Proceedings," 72.

12 Ferguson, *The Trial in American Life*, 272.

13 NPR, "The Eichmann Trial," 1.

14 Ferguson, *The Trial in American Life*, 282.

15 Peabody, "'Supreme Court TV,'" 145.

16 Weiss, "50 State Supreme Courts Allow Cameras, but Not the U.S. Supreme Court," 2.

17 "Illinois Courts, Supreme Court Oral Argument Audio & Video—2017."

18 "Courtroom View Network."

CHAPTER 8

1 Carson and Anderson, *Prisoners in 2015*, 3.

2 Minton and Zeng, *Jail Inmates at Midyear 2014*, 3.

3 Kaeble and Bonczar, *Probation and Parole in the United States, 2015*, 5

4 Probation is a sentence given by the judge to be served in the community; whereas parole is a condition of early release from jail or prison. In this instance, the inmate serves the remainder of his or her sentence in the community.

5 Chermak, "Police, Courts, and Corrections in the Media," 91–92.

6 Surette, *Media, Crime and Criminal Justice*, 136–38.

7 Rafter, *Shots in the Mirror*, 163–69.

8 Eigenberg and Baro, "If You Drop the Soap in the Shower You Are on Your Own," 57.

9 Eigenberg and Baro, "If You Drop the Soap in the Shower You Are on Your Own," 69.

10 Weaver, "The Role of Actors' Race in White Audiences' Selective Exposure to Movies," 370.

11 Shipp, "Refusing to Jail a White Is Called Racist by Koch," 1–4.

12 Surette, *Media, Crime and Criminal Justice*, 138.

13 Jewkes, *Media and Crime*, 206.

14 Jewkes, *Media and Crime*, 209–10.

15 Jewkes, *Media and Crime*, 135–54.

16 Schwan, "Postfeminism Meets the Women in Prison Genre," 474.

17 Jewkes, *Media and Crime*, 207.

18 Sanchez, Hanna, and Martinez, "Joyce Mitchell Pleads Guilty to Helping New York Inmates Escape," 1.

19 Fisher, Allan, and Allan, "Exploratory Study to Examine the Impact of Television Reports of Prison Escapes of Fear of Crime, Operationalised as State Anxiety," 186.

20 Perez, "The Truly Corrosive Problem at Rikers Island," 10.

21 Surette, *Media, Crime and Criminal Justice*, 144.

22 Yousman, *Prime Time Prisons on U.S. TV*, 11.

23 Yousman, *Prime Time Prisons on U.S. TV,* 11.

24 Wilson and O'Sullivan, *Images of Incarceration*, 94.

CHAPTER 9

1 Jurkowitz, et al., "The Changing TV News Landscape," 66.

2 Yousman, *Prime Time Prisons on U.S. TV*, 11.

3 Cullen and Jonson, *Correctional Theory*, 202.

4 Miner, "Body Ritual among the Nacirema," 4–17.

References

ABA. 2016. "Model Rules of Professional Conduct." Last modified 2017. http://www.americanbar.org/groups/professional_responsibility/publications/model_rules_of_professional_conduct/model_rules_of_professional_conduct_table_of_contents.html.

Alforte, Allan. 2016. "Video Games Effects on Child Development: How Bad Is It?" *iTech Post*, December 29. Accessed January 13, 2017. http://www.itechpost.com/articles/69625/20161229/video-games-effects-child-development-bad.htm.

AMC Filmsite. 2017. "Greatest Courtroom Dramas." Last modified 2017. http://www.filmsite.org/.

Amy, Marc T. 2002. "Judiciary School: A Proposal for a Pre-Judicial LL.M. Degree." *Journal of Legal Education* 52(1/2):130–44.

Anderson, Monica, and Andrea Caumont. 2014. "How Social Media Is Reshaping News." Pew Research Center. Accessed December 3, 2015. http://www.pewresearch.org/fact-tank/2014/09/24/how-social-media-is-reshaping-news/.

Ashford, Grace Saffron. 2017. "The Queens Precinct Where Stop-and-Frisk Survives." *Citylimits.org*, January 9. Accessed January 11, 2017. http://citylimits.org/2017/01/09/the-queens-precinct-where-stop-and-frisk-survives/.

Associated Press. 2016. "Oscar Pistorius Sentenced to 6 Years in Prison for Murder of Girlfriend." *Fox News World*, July 6, 2016. Accessed July 6. http://www.foxnews.com/world/2016/07/06/oscar-pistorius-sentenced-to-6-years-in-prison-for-murder-girlfirend.html.

Bainbridge, Jason. 2009. "The Bodies of Law: Performing Truth and the Mythology of Lawyering in American Law Show." *European Journal of Cultural Studies* 12(4):395–415.

Balmas, Meital. 2012. "When Fake News Becomes Real: Combined Exposure to Multiple News Sources and Political Attitudes of Inefficacy, Alienation, and Cynicism." *Communication Research* 41(3):430–54.

Bandura, Albert. 2001. "Social Cognitive Theory of Mass Communication." *Media Psychology* 3:265–99.

Bandura, Albert, Dorothea Ross, and A. Sheila Ross. 1963. "Imitation of Film-Medi ated Aggressive Models." *Journal of Abnormal and Social Psychology* 66(1):3–11.

Barlow, David E., and Melissa H. Barlow. 2000. *Police in a Multicultural Society: An American Story*. Prospect Heights, IL: Waveland Press, Inc.

Belknap, Joanne. 2007. *The Invisible Woman: Gender, Crime and Justice*. 3rd ed. Belmont, CA: Wadsworth.

Bengali, Shashank, and Kate Linthicum. 2015. "San Bernardino Shooter Was a Pakistani Who Became Known as a 'Saudi Girl.'" *Los Angeles Times*, December 17. Accessed January 14, 2017. http://www.latimes.com/world/afghanistan-pakistan/la-fg-malik-profile-20151217-story.html.

Bergen, Peter. 2015. "The Golden Age of Terrorism." *CNN*, August 21. Accessed January 14, 2017. http://www.cnn.com/2015/07/28/opinions/bergen-1970s-terrorism/.

Berrington, Eileen, and Paivi Honkatukia. 2002. "An Evil Monster and a Poor Thing: Female Violence in the Media." *Journal of Scandinavian Studies in Criminology and Crime Prevention* 3:50–72.

Blay, Zeba. 2016. "Black Voices: Let's Not Ignore the Importance of Brock Turner's Whiteness." *Huffington Post*, June 7. Accessed October 4, 2016. http://www.huff ingtonpost.com/entry/lets-not-ignore-the-importance-of-brock-turners-whiteness_us_5756d791e4b0b60682dee518.

Boyd, Susan C. 2007. "Drug Films, Justice, and Nationhood." *Contemporary Justice Review* 10(3):263–82.

Brust, 2008. "The 25 Greatest Legal Movies." *ABA Journal*, August 1. Accessed October 4, 2016. http://www.abajournal.com/magazine/article/the_25_greatest_legal_movies/.

Bult, Laura. 2016. "Former Doctor Convicted of Four Revenge Killings in Omaha." *Daily News*, October 27. Accessed January 12, 2017. http://www.nydailynews.com/news/crime/doctor-convicted-revenge-killings-omaha-article-1.2847502.

Bureau of Labor Statistics. 2016. *American Time Use Survey Summary*. Accessed January 12, 2017. https://www.bls.gov/news.release/atus.nr0.htm.

Campbell, Donald J., and Kathleen M. Campbell. 2010. "Soldiers as Police Officers/Police Officers as Soldiers: Role Evolution and Revolution in the United States." *Armed Forces and Society* 36(2):327–50.

Carson, E. Ann, and Elizabeth Anderson. 2016. *Prisoners in 2015*. Washington, DC: Bureau of Justice Statistics. Accessed April 23, 2017. https://www.bjs.gov/content/pub/pdf/p15.pdf.

Cavender, Gray, and Mark Fishman. 1998. "Television Reality Crime Programs: Context and History." In *Entertaining Crime: Television and Reality Programs*, edited by Mark Fishman and Gray Cavender, 3–15. New York, NY: Aldine De Gruyter.

CBS Detroit. 2015. "2 Accused of Beating up Disabled Man, Posting Video on Facebook." *CBS Detroit*, December 1. Accessed October 4, 2016. http://detroit.cbslocal.com/2015/12/01/2-accused-of-beating-up-disabled-man-posting-video-of-assault-on-facebook/.

CBS News. 2015. "Ferguson State of Emergency Ends after Days of Protests." *CBS News*, August 14. Accessed July 1, 2016. http://www.cbsnews.com/news/ferguson-missouri-state-of-emergency-ends-michael-brown-anniversary-protests/.

CBS News. 2016. "O.J. Simpson Trial: Where Are They Now?" *CBS News*. Accessed July 1, 2016. http://www.cbsnews.com/pictures/the-o-j-simpson-trial-where-are-they-now/.

Chermak, Steven M. 1998. "Police, Courts, and Corrections in the Media." In *Popular Culture, Crime, and Justice*, edited by Frankie Y. Bailey and Donna C. Hale, 87–99. Belmont, CA: West/Wadsworth Publishing Co.

CNN. 2011. "CNN's First Broadcast: June 1, 1980." *CNN*, June 1. Accessed December 3, 2015. http://cnnpressroom.blogs.cnn.com/2011/06/01/cnns-first-broadcast-june-1-1980/.

CNN. 2016. "Complete Coverage on Social Media." *CNN*. Last updated April 23, 2017. http://www.cnn.com/TECH/social.media/archive/.

"Conviction for Arson." 1851. *New-York Daily Times* (1851–1857), October 11, 2.

"Courtroom View Network," Last modified April 21, 2017. http://cvn.com/.

Crime Sider Staff. 2015. "Driver Arrested for Texas Motorcycle Crash Caught on Video." *CBS News.com*, October 20. Accessed October 4, 2016. http://www.cbsnews.com/news/driver-arrested-for-texas-motorcycle-crash-caught-on-video/.

Cullen, Francis T., and Cheryl Lero Jonson. 2017. *Correctional Theory: Context and Consequences*. Los Angeles, CA: Sage Publications, Inc.

Dahl, Julia. 2013. "Trayvon Martin Shooting: A Timeline of Events," *CBS News*, July 12. Accessed September 4, 2016. http://www.cbsnews.com/news/trayvon-martin-shooting-a-timeline-of-events/.

"Dancing Ito's: Can-Can/Apache Dance." *The Tonight Show with Jay Leno*. NBC National Broadcasting Company, NY: NBC, April 27, 1995.

Death Penalty Information Center. 2016. *The Death Penalty in 2016: Year End Report*. Accessed January 11, 2017. http://www.deathpenaltyinfo.org/YearEnd2016.

Durose, Matthew R., and Andrea M. Burch. 2016. *Publicly Funded Forensic Crime Laboratories: Resources and Services, 2014*. Washington, DC: Bureau of Justice Statistics. Accessed April 23, 2017. https://www.bjs.gov/content/pub/pdf/pffclrs14.pdf.

Eigenberg, Helen, and Baro, Agnes. 2003. "If You Drop the Soap in the Shower You Are on Your Own: Images of Male Rapes in Selected Prison Movies." *Sexuality and Culture* 7(4):56–89.

Ellison, Charles D. 2017. "Growing Political Influence of Police Unions Derails Consent Decrees." *The Philadelphia Tribune*, April 15. Accessed January 17, 2017. http://www.phillytrib.com/news/growing-political-influence-of-police-unions-derails-consent-decrees/article_4aec5984-b62c-5004-bd07-2eb9921c12f9.html.

Fasching-Varner, Kenneth J., Rema E. Reynolds, Katrice A. Albert, and Martin, Lori L. (eds). 2014. *Trayvon Martin, Race, and American Justice: Writing Wrong*. Boston, MA: Sense Publishers.

Federal Bureau of Investigation. 2016a. *Crime in the United States, 2015*. Accessed September 18, 2016. https://ucr.fbi.gov/crime-in-the-u.s/2015/crime-in-the-u.s.-2015/offenses-known-to-law-enforcement/violent-crime.

Federal Bureau of Investigation. 2016b. *2015 Crime Clock Statistics*. Accessed January 5, 2017. https://ucr.fbi.gov/crime-in-the-u.s/2015/crime-in-the-u.s.-2015/tables/table-33.

Federal Bureau of Investigation. 2016 "Uniform Crime Reporting," last modified 2017, https://ucr.fbi.gov/.

Fenton, Justin. 2016. "Suspects in Wyman Park Stabbing Filmed the Assault, Posted to Facebook." *The Baltimore Sun*, September 16. Accessed October 4, 2016. http://www.baltimoresun.com/news/maryland/crime/bs-md-ci-stabbing-arrests-20160916-story.html.

Ferguson, Robert A. 2007. *The Trial in American Life*. Chicago, IL: The University of Chicago Press.

Fisher, Sofia, Alfred Allan, and Maria A. Allan. 2004. "Exploratory Study to Examine the Impact of Television Reports of Prison Escapes of Fear of Crime, Operationalised as State Anxiety." *Australian Journal of Psychology* 56(3):181–90.

Foreman, Kelsey, Cecilia Artega, and Aushawna Collins. 2016. "The Role of Media Framing in Crime Reports: How Different Types of News Frames and Racial Identity Affect Viewers' Perceptions of Race." *Pepperdine Journal of Communication Research* 4:8–18.

Fox59. 2017. "3 Suspects Charged in Rape, Abduction at Castleton Hotel." *Fox59*, January 5. Accessed January 5, 2017. http://fox59.com/2017/01/05/3-suspects-charged-in-rape-abduction-at-castleton-hotel-juvenile-claims-he-hears-voices/.

Garcia, Venessa. 2003. "'Difference' in the Police Department: Women, Policing, and 'Doing Gender.'" *Journal of Contemporary Criminal Justice* 19(3):330–44.

Garcia, Venessa. 2005. "Constructing the 'Other' within Police Culture: An Analysis of a Deviant Unit within the Police Organization." *Police Practice and Research* 6(1):65–80.

Garcia, Venessa. 2012. "Constructing and Reconstructing Female Sexual Assault Victims in the Media." In *The Harms of Crime Media: Essays on the Perpetuation of Racism, Sexism and Class Stereotypes*, edited by Denise L. Bissler and Joan L. Conners, 18–37. Jefferson, NC: McFarland Press.

Garcia, Venessa. 2012. "Aileen Wuornos." In *Women Criminals: Encyclopedia of People and Issues,* Vol. 2, edited by Vickie J. Jensen, 641–44. Westport, CT: Greenwood Press.

Garcia, Venessa. 2015. "Snapped: Victimization, Criminals and Crossing the Line." Presented at the Annual Meeting of the Academy of Criminal Justice Science, Orlando, Florida, March 3–7.

Garcia, Venessa. 2017. "Assessing the Current Status of Women in Policing: The Presence of the Past." In *Change and Reform in Law Enforcement: Old and New Efforts from Across the Globe*, edited by Scott W. Phillips and Dilip K. Das, 171–88. Boca Raton, FL: CRC Press.

Garcia, Venessa, and Liqun Cao. 2005. "Race and Satisfaction with the Police in a Small City." *Journal of Criminal Justice* 33:191–99.

Garcia, Venessa, and Richard Butler. 2005. "White Collar Crime Enforcement." In *Encyclopedia of Law Enforcement,* Vol. 2, edited by Larry E. Sullivan and Dorothy Moses Schulz, 904–08. Thousand Oaks, CA: Sage Publications.

Gerstenfeld, Phyllis B. 2013. *Hate Crime: Causes, Control and Controversies*. 3rd ed. Thousand Oaks, CA: Sage Publications, Inc.

Gilboa, Eytan. 2005. "The CNN Effect: The Search for a Communication Theory of International Relation." *Political Communications* 22(1):27–44.

Gingras, Brynn, Sonia Moghe, and Emanuella Grinberg. 2017. "Quick-Thinking McDonald's Worker Leads Police to Facebook Killer." *CNN*, April 19. Accessed April 22, 2017. http://www.cnn.com/2017/04/18/us/mcdonalds-employee-identify-facebook-killer/.

Gottfried, Jeffrey, and Elisa Shearer. 2016. "News Use across Social Media Platforms 2016." Pew Research Center. Accessed July 13, 2016. http://www.journalism. org/2016/05/26/news-use-across-social-media-platforms-2016/.

Graziano, Lisa, Amie Schuck, and Christine Martin. 2010. "Police Misconduct, Media Coverage, and Public Perceptions of Racial Profiling: An Experiment." *Justice Quarterly* 27(1):52–76.

Grinberg, Emanuella, and Catherine E. Sholchet. 2016. "Brock Turner Released from Jail after Serving 3 Months for Sexual Assault." *CNN*, September 2. Accessed October 4, 2016. http://www.cnn.com/2016/09/02/us/brock-turner-release-jail/.

Grossberg, Lawrence, Ellen Wartella, and D. Charles Whitney. 1998. *MediaMaking: Mass Media in a Popular Culture*. Thousand Oaks, CA: Sage Publications, Inc.

Hamilton, James T. 1998. *Channeling Violence: The Economic Market for Violent Television Programming*. Princeton, NJ: Princeton University Press.

Hapke, Laura. 1989. *Girls Who Went wrong: Prostitutes in American Fiction, 1885–1917*. Bowling Green, OH: Bowling Green State University Popular Press.

Harrell, Erika, 2013. *Workplace Violence against Government Employees, 1994–2011*. U.S. Department of Justice. Accessed April 20, 2017. https://www.bjs.gov/content/pub/pdf/wvage9411.pdf.

Harris, Charlaine. 2016. "Charlaine Harris." Last modified June 17, 2016. http://charlaineharris.com/?s=teagarden.

Helfield, Randa. 1995. "Poisonous Plots: Women Sensation Novelists and Murderesses of the Victorian Period." *Victorian Review* 21(2):161–88.

History.com Staff. 2009. "Columbine High School Shootings." *History.com*. Last modified July 8, 2016. http://www.history.com/topics/columbine-high-school-shootings.

Hixson, Walter L. 2001. *Murder, Culture, and Injustice: Four Sensational Cases in American History*. Akron, OH: The University of Akron Press.

Hu, Winnie, 2016. "6 Ex-Rikers Guards Sentenced to Prison in Attack on Inmate." *The New York Times*, September 16. Accessed September 18, 2016. http://www. nytimes.com/2016/09/17/nyregion/rikers-island-officers-sentencing-jahmal-light foot-beating.html?_r=0.

"Illinois Courts, Supreme Court Oral Argument Audio & Video—2017." Last modified April 21, 2017. http://www.illinoiscourts.gov/Media/On_Demand.asp.

IMDB, 2017. "Top-US-Grossing Crime Titles." IMDB. Accessed April 12, 2017. http://www.imdb.com/search/title?genres=crime&page=1&view=advanced&sort= moviemeter,asc&ref_=adv_prv.

Innocence Project. 2016. "Innocence Project." Last modified 2016. http://www.inno cenceproject.org/about/.

Innocence Project. 2017. "Exonerate the Innocent." Last modified 2017. https://www. innocenceproject.org/exonerate/.

Jewkes, Yvonne. 2011. *Media and Crime: Key Approaches to Criminology*. 2nd ed. Thousand Oaks, CA: Sage Publications.

Jockel, Sven, and Hannah Fruh. 2016. "'The World Ain't All Sunshine': Investigating the Relationship between Mean World Beliefs, Conservatism and Crime TV Exposure." *Communications* 41(2):195–217.

Johnson, Lyndon B. 1966. "Special Message to the Congress on Crime and Law Enforcement." *The American Presidency Project*, March 9. Accessed August 2, 2016. http://www.presidency.ucsb.edu/ws/?pid=27478.

Joseph, Philip. 2013. "Soldiers in Baltimore: The Wire and the New Global Wars." *The New Centennial Review* 13(1):209–40.

Jurkowitz, Mark, Paul Hitlin, Amy Mitchell, Laura Santhanam, Steve Adams, Monica Anderson, and Nancy Vogt. 2013. "The State of the News Media 2013: An Annual Report on American Journalism." *The Pew Research Center's Project for Excellence in Journalism*. Accessed April 18, 2017. http://www.stateofthemedia.org/2013/special-reports-landing-page/the-changing-tv-news-landscape/.

Kaeble, Danielle, and Thomas P. Bonczar. 2016. *Probation and Parole in the United States, 2015*. Washington, DC: Bureau of Justice Statistics. Accessed April 20, 2017, https://www.bjs.gov/content/pub/pdf/ppus15.pdf.

Kaeble, Danielle, Laura M. Maruschak, and Thomas P. Bonczar, 2015. *Probation and Parole in the United States, 2014*. Bureau of Justice Statistics. Accessed September 18, 2016. http://www.bjs.gov/index.cfm?ty=pbdetail&iid=5415.

Kang, Cecilia. 2016. "Fake News Onslaught Targets Pizzeria as Nest of Child-Trafficking." *The New York Times*, November 21. Accessed January 1, 2017. http://www.nytimes.com/2016/11/21/technology/fact-check-this-pizzeria-is-not-a-child-trafficking-site.html.

Kaplan, Michael. 2016. "Why Violent Video Games Are Good for Kids." *New York Post*, December 19. Accessed January 13, 2017. http://nypost.com/2016/12/19/why-violent-video-games-are-good-for-kids/.

Keating, Patrick. 2010. *Hollywood Lighting from the Silent Era to Film Noir*. New York, NY: Columbia University Press.

Kimble, Julian. 2014. "Memories of a Massacre: What We've Learned 15 Years After Columbine," *Complex Pop Culture*, April 20. Accessed January 11, 2017. http://www.complex.com/pop-culture/2014/04/what-we-ve-learned-15-years-after-columbine-shootings.

King, Shaun. 2016. "Brock Turner, Corey Batey Show How Race Affects Sentencing." *Daily News*, June 7. Accessed October 4, 2016. http://www.nydailynews.com/news/national/king-brock-turner-cory-batey-show-race-affects-sentencing-article-1.2664945.

Kinlay, Alicia. 2010. "Televised Court Proceedings: The Relationship between the Media, Punitive Public Perceptions and Populist Party." *Flinders Journal of History and Politics* 26:71–85.

Lacey-Bordeaux, Emma. 2016. "Police Rescue Autistic Boy's Birthday Party." *CNN*, August 10. Accessed October 18, 2016. http://www.cnn.com/2016/08/10/health/police-autistic-boy-birthday-party-trnd/.

Langton, Lynn. 2010. *Women in Law Enforcement, 1987–2008*. Washington, DC: Bureau of Justice Statistics. Accessed April 23, 2017. https://www.bjs.gov/content/pub/pdf/wle8708.pdf.

Lichtblau, Eric. 2009. *Bush's Law: The Remaking of American Justice*. New York, NY: Anchor Books.

Lubbers, Eric. 2016. "There is No Such Thing as the Denver Guardian, Despite that Facebook Post You Saw," *The Denver Post*, November 6. Accessed January 11, 2017. http://www.denverpost.com/2016/11/05/there-is-no-such-thing-as-the-denver-guardian/.

Lysiak, Matthew. 2014. "Why Adam Lanza Did It." *Newsweek*, January 17. Accessed January 14, 2017. http://www.newsweek.com/why-adam-lanza-did-it-226565.

Maeder, Evelyn M., and Richard Corbett. 2015. "Beyond Frequency: Perceived Realism and the *CSI* Effect." *Canadian Journal of Criminology and Criminal Justice* 57(1):83–114.

Mahashari, Sapna. 2016. "How Fake News Goes Viral: A Case Study." *The New York Times*, November 20. Accessed January 4, 2017. http://www.nytimes.com/2016/11/20/business/media/how-fake-news-spreads.html?_r=0&register=google.

Mallicoat, Stacy L., and Connie E. Ireland. 2014. *Women and Crime: The Essentials*. Los Angeles, CA: Sage Publications, Inc.

Marsh, Julia. 2017. "Revenge Porn Victim to Google: Make Me Disappear." *New York Post*, January 3. Accessed January 12, 2017. http://nypost.com/2017/01/03/revenge-porn-victim-wants-her-name-deleted-from-google/.

Martinez, Michael. 2015. "South Carolina Cop Shoots Unarmed Man: A Timeline." *CNN*, April 9. Accessed March 15, 2016. http://www.cnn.com/2015/04/08/us/south-carolina-cop-shoots-black-man-timeline/.

McLaughlin, Michael, 2013. "Murders, Shootings and Gun Sales per Day: An Average Day in United States." *The Huffington Post*, January 16. Accessed September 18, 2016. http://www.huffingtonpost.com/2013/01/16/murders-shootings-and-gun-sales-per-day_n_2488664.html.

McNamara, Melissa. 2006. "Lionel Tate Gets 30 Years in Jail." *CBS News*, May 18. Accessed July 13, 2016. http://www.cbsnews.com/news/lionel-tate-gets-30-years-in-jail/.

Miller, Wilbur R. (2012). "Primary Document 1930: The Motion Picture Production Code of 1930." In *The Social History of Crime and Punishment in America: An Encyclopedia*, edited by Wilbur R. Miller, 2224–26. Los Angeles, CA: Sage Publications, Inc.

Miner, Horace. 1956. "Body Ritual among the Nacirema." *American Anthropologist* 58:503–07. Accessed April 18, 2017. https://msu.edu/~jdowell/miner.html#1.

Minton, Todd D., and Zhen Zeng. 2015. *Jail Inmates at Midyear 2014*. Washington DC: Bureau of Justice Statistics. Accessed April 23, 2017. https://www.bjs.gov/content/pub/pdf/jim14.pdf.

Morin, Aysel. 2016. "Framing Terror: The Strategies Newspapers Use to Frame an Act as Terror or Crime." *Journalism & Mass Communication Quarterly* 93(4): 986–1005.

Morton, Robert J., Jennifer M. Tillman, and Stephanie J. Gaines. (2014). *Serial Murder: Pathways for Investigations*. Washington, DC: Justice Department. Accessed February 12, 2017. file:///E:/Research/Rowman&Littlefield/Sources/Ch5_Articles/SerialMurder-PathwaysForInvestigations.pdf.

Muraskin, Roslyn, and Shelly Feuer Domash. 2007. *Crime and the Media: Headline versus Reality*. Upper Saddle River, NJ: Pearson Education, Inc.

Murphy, Doyle. 2015. "Pennsylvania Man Kills Toddler in WWE Wrestling Imitation." *Daily News*, May 7. Accessed January 13, 2017. http://www.nydailynews.com/news/national/pennsylvania-man-kills-toddler-wwe-wrestling-imitation-article-1.2214628.

Murphy, Priscilla. 2010. "The Intractability of Reputation: Media Coverage as a Complex System in the Case of Martha Stewart." *Journal of Public Relations Research* 22(2):209–37.

Neubauer, David W., and Henry F. Fradella. 2011. *American's Courts and the Criminal Justice System*. 10th ed. Belmont, CA: Wadsworth, Cengage Learning.

Nielson. 2016. "Tops of 2016: TV." Last modified February 3, 2017. http://www.nielsen.com/us/en/insights/news/2016/tops-of-2016-tv.html.

Nielsen. 2017. "Top Ten." Last modified February 3, 2017. http://www.nielsen.com/us/en/top10s.html.

Nordheimer, Jon. 1994. "Youth, 14, Draws 9 Years to Life in Killing of 4-Year-Old." *The New York Times*, November 8. Accessed July 6, 2016. http://www.nytimes.com/1994/11/08/nyregion/youth-14-draws-9-years-to-life-in-killing-of-4-year-old.html.

NPR. 2011. "The Eichmann Trial: Fifty Years Later." NPR, March 27. Accessed February 24, 2017, http://www.npr.org/2011/03/27/134821325/the-eichmann-trial-fifty-years-later.

Office of the Historian. N.d. "U.S. Diplomacy and Yellow Journalism, 1895–1898." Accessed April 30, 2016. https://history.state.gov/milestones/1866-1898/yellow-journalism.

Oliver, Mary Beth, and G. Blake Armstrong. 1998. "The Color of Crime: Perceptions of Caucasians' and African-Americans' Involvement in Crime." In *Entertaining Crime: Television and Reality Programs*, edited by Mark Fishman and Gray Cavender, 19–35. New York, NY: Aldine De Gruyter.

Paul, Angelique M. 1997. "Turning on the Camera on Court TV: Does Televising Trials Teach Us Anything about the Real Law." *Ohio State Law Journal* 58(5):655–694.

Peabody, Bruce G. 2017. "'Supreme Court TV': Televising the Least Accountable Branch?" *Journal of Legislation* 33(2):144–80.

Perez, Johnny. 2017. "The Truly Corrosive Problem at Rikers Island." *Daily News*, April 9. Accessed April 14, 2017, http://www.nydailynews.com/opinion/corrosive-problem-rikers-island-article-1.3035659.

Pollock, Joycelyn M. 2008. "Whatever Happened to Atticus Finch? Lawyers as Legal Advocates and Moral Agents." In *Justice, Crime and Ethics*, 6th ed., edited by Michael C. Braswell, Belinda R. McCarthy, and Bernard J. McCarthy, 133–48. Newark, NJ: LexisNexis Group.

Pooley, Eric. 1989. "Grins, Gore, and Videotape: The Trouble with Local TV News." *New York Magazine*, October 9, 36–44. Accessed April 23, 2017. https://books.google.com/books?id=_OcCAAAAMBAJ&pg=PA36&source=gbs_toc_r&cad=2#v=onepage&q&f=false.

Prokupecz, Shimon, and Kevin Conlon. 2014. "NYPD: Hatchet Attack an Act of Terror." *CNN*, November 5. Accessed January 14, 2017. http://www.cnn.com/2014/10/24/us/new-york-police-attacked/.

Rafter, Nicole. 2006. *Shots in the Mirror*. 2nd ed. New York, NY: Oxford University Press.

Rafter, Nicole, and Michelle Brown. 2011. *Criminology Goes to the Movies: Crime Theory and Popular Culture*. New York, NY: New York University Press.

Rakes, Amanda. 2015. "Indiana Woman Arrested after Father Records Video of Alleged Child Abuse, Posts it on Facebook." *Fox 59*, December 3. Accessed October 4, 2016. http://fox59.com/2015/12/03/police-indiana-father-records-woman-abusing-kids-posts-it-on-facebook/.

Ray, Robert Beverley. 1985. *A Certain Tendency of the Hollywood Cinema, 1930–1980*. Princeton, NJ: Princeton University Press.

Reaves, Brian. 2012. *Hiring and Retention of State and Local Law Enforcement Officers, 2008 Statistical Tables*. Washington, DC: Bureau of Justice Statistics. Accessed April 23, 2017. https://www.bjs.gov/content/pub/pdf/hrslleo08st.pdf.

Rizun, Sarah. 2012. "Fictionalized Women in Trouble: An Exploration of the Television Crime Drama CSI: Miami." In *The Harms of Crime Media: Essays on the Perpetuation of Racism, Sexism and Class Stereotypes*, edited by Denise L. Bissler and Joan L. Conners, 190–207. Jefferson, NC: McFarland & Co., Inc., Publishers.

Robinson, Matthew B. 2014. *Media Coverage of Crime and Criminal Justice*. 2nd ed. Durham, NC: Carolina Academic Press.

Rosenbaum, Thane. 2016. "The 6 Types of Lawyer Movies: Movie Trope Trading Cards." *ABA Journal* 102(8):44–50. Accessed April 16, 2017. http://draweb.njcu.edu:2118/ps/i.do?p=AONE&u=jers45639&id=GALE|A464758824&v=2.1&it=r&sid=summon&authCount=1.

Ross, T. Cody. 2015. "A Multi-Level Bayesian Analysis of Racial Bias in Police Shootings at the County-Level in the United States, 2011–2014." *PLOS/One*. Accessed February 24, 2017. http://journals.plos.org/plosone/article?id=10.1371/journal.pone.0141854#sec005.

Sanchez, Ray, Jason Hanna, and Michael Martinez. 2015. "Joyce Mitchell Pleads Guilty to Helping New York Inmates Escape." *CNN*, July 29. Accessed April 14, 2017. http://www.cnn.com/2015/07/28/us/new-york-prison-break-mitchell/.

Sasson, Theodore. 1995. *Crime Talk: How Citizens Construct a Social Problem*. New York, NY: Aldine De Gruyter.

Schwan, Anne. 2016. "Postfeminism Meets the Women in Prison Genre: Privilege and Spectatorship in *Orange Is the New Black*." *Television & New Media* 17(16):473–90.

Schwartz, A. Brad. 2015. *Broadcast Hysteria: Orson Welles's War of the Worlds and the Art of Fake News*. New York, NY: Hill and Wang.

Schwartz, Danny. 2016. "10 Best Hip Hop Protest Songs since the Trayvon Martin Shooting." *Hot New Hip Hop*, July 8. Accessed September 4, 2016. http://www.hotnewhiphop.com/the-10-best-hip-hop-protest-songs-since-the-trayvon-martin-shooting-news.22741.html.

Seewer, John. 2017. "How Police Departments with Consent Decrees Are Faring." *PoliceOne.com*. Accessed April 15, 2017. https://www.policeone.com/doj/articles/324031006-How-police-departments-with-consent-decrees-are-faring/.

Shipp, E. R. 1981. "Refusing to Jail a White Is Called Racist by Koch." *The New York Times*, April 10. Accessed April 14, 2017. http://www.nytimes.com/1981/04/10/nyregion/refusing-to-jail-a-white-is-called-racist-by-koch.html.

Stabile, Carol A. 2004. "Getting What She Deserved: The News Media, Martha Stewart, and Masculine Domination." *Feminist Media Studies* 4(3):315–32.

Statista, 2017. N.d. "Global Box Office Revenue from 2016 to 2020." Accessed April 20, 2017, https://www.statista.com/statistics/259987/global-box-office-revenue/.

Stevens, Dennis J. 2011. *Media and Criminal Justice: The CSI Effect*. Sudbury, MA: Jones and Bartlett Publishers.

Surette, Ray. 1998. "Prologue: Some Unpopular Thoughts about Popular Culture." In *Popular Culture, Crime, and Justice*, edited by Frankie Bailey and Donna Hale, xiv–xxiv. Belmont, CA: West/Wadsworth Publishing Co.

Surette, Ray. 2015. *Media, Crime and Criminal Justice: Images, Realities, and Policies*. 5th ed. Belmont, CA: Wadsworth.

Svetkey, Benjamin. 1991. "Introducing Court TV." *Entertainment*, August 2. Accessed February 25, 2017. http://ew.com/article/1991/08/02/introducing-court-tv/.

Sweeney, Annie, Steve Schmadeke, and Jason Meisner. 2017. "How to Stop Guns, Gangs and Poverty? Chicago Seeks Solutions After Violent 2016." *Chicago Tribune*, January 1. Accessed January 11, 2017. http://www.chicagotribune.com/news/ct-chicago-violence-solutions-met-20161230-story.html.

Tate, Julie, Jennifer Jenkins, and Steven Rich. 2015. "Fatal Force." *The Washington Post*. Last modified April 15, 2017, https://www.washingtonpost.com/graphics/national/police-shootings-2016/.

"TheRightists.com." Last modified 2015. http://therightists.com/about-us/.

Thielking, Megan. 2017. "Gun Violence Spreads Like an Infectious Disease, New Research Finds." *PBS Newshour*, January 4. Accessed January 12, 2017. http://www.pbs.org/newshour/rundown/gun-violence-infectious-disease-research/.

Today. 2016. "Share Your Visit." Last modified April 23, 2017. http://visit.today.com/share-your-visit/.

Tonry, Michael H. 2011. *Punishing Race: A Continuing American Dilemma*. New York: Oxford University Press.

Trask, Steven. 2016. "The Shocking Moment a Homeless Man Attacks a Woman with a Wooden Stake on a Busy Street in Melbourne." *Daily Mail Australia*, May 9. Accessed June 23, 2016. http://www.dailymail.co.uk/news/article-3581035/Homeless-man-attacks-Melbourne-woman-garden-stake-St-Kilda.html.

Turnbull, Sue. 2010. "Crime as Entertainment: The Case of the TV Crime Drama." *Continuum: Journal of Media & Cultural Studies* 24(6):819–27.

Turow, Joseph. 2014. *Media Today: Mass Communication in a Converging World*. 5th ed. New York, NY: Routledge.

Valenzuela, Sebastian, and Angela S. Brandao. 2015. "Historical Dramas, Current Political Choices: Analyzing Partisan Selective Exposure with a Docudrama." *Mass Communication and Society* 18:449–70.

Vester, Katharina. 2015. "Bodies to Die for: Negating the Ideal Female Body in Cozy Mystery Novels." *Journal of Popular Culture* 48:31–43.

"Volunteers." *Law & Order*. NBC National Broadcasting Co., NY: NBC, September 29, 1993.

Washington Post Staff. 2015. "Full Text: Donald Trump Announces a Presidential Bid." *The Washington Post*, June 16. Accessed January 4, 2017. https://www.

washingtonpost.com/news/post-politics/wp/2015/06/16/full-text-donald-trump-announces-a-presidential-bid/?utm_term=.e6705f66512b.

Weaver, Andrew J. 2011. "The Role of Actors' Race in White Audiences' Selective Exposure to Movies." *Journal of Communication* 62(2):369–85.

Websdale, Neil, and Alexander Alvarez. 1998. "Forensic Journalism as Patriarchal Ideology: The Newspaper Construction of Homicide-Suicide." In *Popular Culture, Crime, and Justice*, edited by Frankie Bailey and Donna Hale, 126–28. Belmont, CA: West/Wadsworth Publishing Co.

Weiss, Debra Cassens. 2013. "50 State Supreme Courts Allow Cameras, but Not the U.S. Supreme Court, Is It a 'fragile flower'?" *ABA Journal*, October 28. Accessed April 3, 2017. http://www.abajournal.com/news/article/50_state_supreme_courts_allow_cameras_but_not_the_us_supreme_court_is_it_a_/.

Welch, Michael, Melissa Fenwick, and Meredith Roberts. 1998. "State Managers, Intellectuals, and the Media." *Justice Quarterly* 15(2):219–41.

Wilson, David, and Sean O'Sullivan. 2004. *Images of Incarceration: Representations of Prison in Film and Television Drama*. Winchester, UK: Waterside Press.

Yousman, Bill. 2009. *Prime Time Prisons on U.S. TV: Representation of Incarceration*. New York, NY: Peter Lang Publishing.

Zgoba, Kristen, Philip Witt, Melissa Dalessandro, and Bonita Veysey. 2008. *Megan's Law: Assessing the Practical and Monetary Efficacy*. Washington, DC: U.S. Department of Justice. Accessed April 23, 2017. https://www.ncjrs.gov/pdffiles1/nij/grants/225370.pdf.

Image Credits

Subject Index

About the Authors

Venessa Garcia earned her doctorate in sociology from the State University of New York at Buffalo in 1999 and is a full-time member of the faculty with the Department of Criminal Justice at New Jersey City University. Dr. Garcia's research focus is in the areas of women and crime justice as well as crime and media. Her media research has been published in books and encyclopedias. She has published research on women, race, and policing in academic journals. Dr. Garcia's previous book was titled, *Gendered Justice: Intimate Partner Violence and the Criminal Justice System*, also with Rowman & Littlefield. She also published a book on female victims of crime. Dr. Garcia is currently working on books in the areas of women and policing and female offenders.

Samantha Garcia Arkerson is a student of early childhood development. When not working with children, she enjoys writing short stories, drawing, and photography. Her art was displayed at the Union County Teen Arts Festival, and she has been commissioned on other art projects. Samantha brings to this book a generational perspective.